ROCKING FATHERHOOD

Rocking
FATHERHOOD

The Dad-to-Be's Guide to Staying Cool

Chris Kornelis

Illustrations by Aaron Bagley

Da Capo

LIFE LONG

A Member of the Perseus Books Group

Copyright © 2016 by Chris Kornelis

Illustrations by Aaron Bagley

Some portions of this book originally appeard in *Seattle Weekly* and on SeattleWeekly.com and TheAtlantic.com.

Designed by Cynthia Young
Set in 10.5 point Palatino LT Std

Cataloging-in-Publication data for this book is available from the Library of Congress.
First Da Capo Press edition 2016
ISBN: 978-0-7382-1877-9 (paperback)
ISBN: 978-0-7382-1878-6 (e-book)

Published by Da Capo Press
A Member of the Perseus Books Group
www.dacapopress.com

Da Capo Press books are available at special discounts for bulk purchases in the U.S. by corporations, institutions, and other organizations. For more information, please contact the Special Markets Department at the Perseus Books Group, 2300 Chestnut Street, Suite 200, Philadelphia, PA, 19103, or call (800) 810-4145, ext. 5000, or e-mail special.markets@perseusbooks.com.

10 9 8 7 6 5 4 3 2 1

For Betsy Kornelis and Laura Kornelis
Dedicated mothers, patient wives

Contents

Foreword by Duff McKagan . . . . *ix*

Preface . . . . *xiii*

Weeks 1 to 4: Clean Yourself Up First 1

Week 5: You Don't "Need" a Bigger Place 6

Week 6: Hang Onto Your Stereo and Record Collection. 11

Week 7: In Defense of Selling Out 15

Week 8: What to Expect When She's Reading
What to Expect 26

Week 9: Ask Her What You Can Be Doing Better. 30

Week 10: Respect Yourself: Don't Carry a Diaper Bag. 33

Week 11: Safe Sex Is Great Sex 40

Week 12: Lose Weight Before the Sympathy Weight
(Otherwise, Buy a Vest). 44

Week 13: Fight for the Fatherhood You Want for
Your Family 47

Week 14: Watch Out for Depression. 58

Week 15: Don't Let Her Microwave Bologna 62

Week 16: Having a Baby Doesn't Change Everything. 66

Week 17: Yes, Swaddling Is a Sport 75

Week 18: Shush Your Way to the Happiest Baby
on the Block 79

Week 19: You Can Take It With You 82

Week 20: Listen to Laura Veirs 91

Week 21: Listen to Caspar Babypants 96

Week 22: It's OK. Nobody Else Knows How They're
Going to Make It Work, Either.. .. .. .100

Week 23: You Can Do Better, Even If You've Never
Seen It Done Before .. .. .113

Week 24: You Can't Properly Install a Car Seat Unless
You've Seen It Done Before .. .. .119

Week 25: Consider the Formula. .. .. .124

Week 26: Pick a Pediatrician You Actually Like .. .. .138

Week 27: Don't Be Afraid to Be an Asshole .. .. .142

Week 28: Walk, Don't Run: Giving Birth Isn't Like It Is
On TV.. .. .. .147

Week 29: You Don't Need a Six-Week Birthing Course
(Only a 3x5 Card) .. .. .153

Week 30: But, of Course, Take the Birthing Course.. .. .. .. .158

Week 31: Just Do Everything Yourself .. .. .161

Week 32: Make Time for the Two of You .. .. .164

Week 33: Forget the Garden, Get a Crock-Pot 169

Week 34: Free Time Isn't a Luxury. It's a Necessity .. .. .. .176

Week 35: There Will Be a Parent Running Point
(The Other One Is Helping).. .. .. .182

Week 36: To Paternity Leave (and Beyond!) 186

Week 37: Take Studies, Recommendations,
and (Especially) Books With a Grain of Salt .. .. .194

Week 38: A Small List For the Big Day .. .. .199

Week 39: A Small List for the Next Day .. .. .202

Weeks 40 to 947: No Child Has Ever Been
Brought Up Right .. .. .206

Postscript .. .. .213

Acknowledgments. .. .. .217

Notes 219

Index 231

Foreword by Duff McKagan

When it comes to pregnancy and rearing children, we men have been left to figure things out on our own. There's little in the way of "how-to" books for us. All of the attention goes to the woman for nine months while she's pregnant and giving birth, and then that's just sort of that.

We were once boys, and then young men—wild and free, we perhaps saved a little space in the brain for the "what if?" of one day having children. And then, all of a sudden for us future dads, reality sets in. Our significant other is pregnant and we all hurriedly do our homework, cram for the test, and try to grapple with what the hell is coming next. *How does a guy change a diaper?!* is only one of the millions of thoughts that go through our heads.

I remember reading *What To Expect When You're Expecting* when my wife was pregnant with our first daughter. I also remember being, frankly, quite freaked-the-fuck out. There didn't seem to be a lot of good information out there specifically for me, the expectant dad. Would I be a good father? What does being a good dad mean? My wife is glaring at me like she wants to stab me in the neck, and I didn't do anything differently today to warrant that look! Could I provide for this growing family? Are we living in the right neighborhood? Will my car get us home from the hospital without, I dunno, something freakish like the axle splitting in two? All of these thoughts and many more, I was left to figure out.

My relationship with Chris Kornelis goes back to before he and Betsy had their first child, Thomas. Chris was my editor at *Seattle Weekly*, and we became good friends throughout our five years of working together. He would call me when Betsy was pregnant and ask me a ton of questions. I did my best to guide him through the things I knew about and had experience with, and I could tell that he was dealing with many of the same questions and doubts that I had as an expectant father.

At some point during our many talks about being dads, Chris simply stated that it was about time there was a book for us— expectant fathers. I heartily agreed, and lo and behold, he wrote that damn book!

Well researched and written with a funny wit during Betsy's second pregnancy, Mr. Kornelis's book cuts straight to the real stuff that we fellas need to know. I truly believe Chris Kornelis has written a book for the ages, one that's extremely readable and undeniably funny. At last, future fathers, you have a tome of your own.

Duff McKagan is the author of How to Be a Man: (and other illusions), *and a cofounder of Guns N' Roses*

Preface

I'm going to make an admission here that might not only em-
barrass my family, but also confirm your suspicion that I have
no business writing a book about pregnancy, fatherhood, or any
other subject that requires critical thinking and study. But I'm going to make this admission for a couple reasons: the first is that
asking stupid questions as an antidote to ignorance is a sign of
next-level parenting. It doesn't take any credentials to become

a parent. Any game couple with a bottle of cheap whiskey and spare time qualifies. But it's a sign of sophistication and self-confidence to ask for help. Don't feel bad when you have to raise your hand. Pat yourself on the back. Buy yourself a drink. Tweet that shit.

The second reason is that I feel better when I profess my ignorance. I come from a profession in which publicly rectifying one's ignorance is seen as a sign of weakness. I learned this when I was fifteen, during my first job in the "music industry."

I spent two years in the late nineties working at Poulsbo Music, a store that sold guitars, LPs, and clarinet reeds. This was during the time Sean Combs was going by the handle "Puff Daddy," and I vividly remember asking the shop owner's son to tell me which part of "Come With Me" was cribbed from Led Zeppelin's "Kashmir": the music or the lyrics. He responded by asking me what kind of musical moron his father had hired to sweep the floors.

As I progressed in the "industry," and found my way to music journalism, I've kept that moment close. I can count on one hand the number of times I've asked, "Who are we listening to?" I'm petrified that the answer will be: "Led Zeppelin! What kind of musical moron are you?" Every music writer feels this way. We won't all admit it. But we're all self-conscious to a fault.

So, here we go, I'm going to make my confession: until about seven or eight weeks ago, I didn't know what torticollis was. Please be merciful and hold your scorn. I'm sure you know what it is, but for those of you who don't—no, it's not on *Zeppelin III*—I'll start at the beginning.

By the third month of my daughter Lucy's life, my family—me, Betsy, our son Thomas—was head over heels for our new baby. She was sleeping through the night like a champ, and generally injecting healthy rays of light into our lives. One day Betsy asked me whether I noticed that she always looked to the right. I guess I hadn't.

I checked it out and saw that, yeah, Lucy really liked turning to the right. It wasn't that Lucy *couldn't* hang a Lucy in that Derek Zoolander kind of way. I could get her to look left, but then she'd snap back to the right. She didn't appear to be in any pain. She just seriously favored the right.

At Lucy's next doctor's appointment, Betsy demonstrated Lu's preference for her starboard side, and the doctor seemed . . . not concerned, but interested. He prescribed a lot of tummy time (exactly what it sounds like) and said that if the situation didn't start to improve soon, he would prescribe some physical therapy. After a few weeks of less than moderate improvement, Betsy made an appointment with a physical therapist.

Long story short, Lucy was probably looking to the right in the womb, and was born with a serious crick in her neck, also known as torticollis. The therapist wasn't alarmed. She expected Lucy to make a full recovery and lead a happy and healthy life. And, since then, she has.

Now, you may be thinking that I should have been aware of torticollis *before* Lucy was born so that on the off chance she had it I would know what to do. Well, don't. I'm glad I didn't know what torticollis was two months ago, and I'm mildly upset that I've told you what it is now, because it's the kind of thing so many parents think they need to know, but don't. It's another brick in the wall of information expectant parents are confronted with and feel the need to absorb.

Pregnancy and parenthood have become minefields of industry and alarmism, which is why expectant parents hear "having a baby changes everything" more often than "having a baby is pure joy." The unrelenting barrage of recommendations and recipes for optimization has added layers of shame and guilt onto an already anxiety-soaked time of life. It's made pregnancy seem like a cataclysmic medical emergency and parenthood seem like a chore. Worst of all, it's made women—who field the brunt of all of the above—feel like inadequate mothers.

I've got a chapter, more or less, for each week of pregnancy, but don't expect a primer on every statistic and scenario that you and your lady could plausibly encounter over the next nine months. That's not what I'm trying to do. I'm trying to give you the basic information you need to care for an infant during the first days of his life and provide you with the ammunition you need to protect your lady during the time in her life when friends, family members, strangers, and statisticians are telling her that they know what's best for her body.

But pregnancy is not only about a woman giving birth. It's also about families transitioning. Men today are making different transitions than their fathers did. We have different opportunities and challenges. In the pages that follow, I use my own experiences (cautionary tales?) to tip you off to some of the conversations, situations, and roadblocks ahead. I don't attempt to give you a template for what's right. Rather, I hope to encourage you to make decisions based on what you think is best for your family, not to conform to someone else's definition of ideal.

There are plenty of things about pregnancy and fatherhood that I've left out. That's because I want to be of as little help as possible while still being helpful. I believe you only need to know a few things before you bring your baby home from the hospital and advance into fatherhood. Your instincts will take care of the rest.

Don't worry, if something goes awry, there will be paid professionals and a bounty of literature at your disposal. Don't burden yourself with mastering it all now.

If you think that being advised to rein in the reconnaissance is a bit suspect coming from a guy who can't recite all the lyrics to "Kashmir" and can't spell *torticollis*, consider two pieces of wisdom I recently received from a pair of gentlemen imminently more qualified than myself. The first came from my childhood pediatrician, Dr. Gregory E. Keyes.

"If our survival were dependent on what, exactly, we fed our kids or whether we breast fed them for nine months or longer, or whether we did certain behaviors when we came home from the hospital, none of us would be here, none of us would survive. It really is more about loving your kids and sitting back and enjoying them. If the child feels loved and accepted and listened to, then everything else will fall into place."

The second came from Dr. David Hill, an officer at the American Academy of Pediatrics. When I read him the above quote from Dr. Keyes, he perked up and added a P.S.

"I would add that every now and then, we figure out something that really is important. Knowing what those things are matters. For example: vaccines, that's a really big deal. Car seats: That's really important. The back to sleep campaign—that's really a big deal. Sudden infant deaths fell by 50 percent when we learned that infants should be sleeping on their backs, not on their stomachs. So, I think it's important that doctors talking to parents and parents talking to doctors distinguish between the things that are a big deal and the things that are not a really big deal."

This book is about the things that are a really big deal. Your instincts, in-laws, and Google will take care of the rest.

Weeks 1 to 4

Clean Yourself Up First

Your baby has just made her presence known.

Your lady is emotional. And so are you.

The situation: You just found out you're going to be a father. There are a million things you feel like you should be doing to prepare.

The reality: Start simple: clean yourself up first.

*T*homas wore the first diaper I ever changed. Six hours old, he cried in horror, his cheeks bright red below his blue, hospital-issued skullcap. I beamed.

The first relief of fatherhood is the realization that changing diapers isn't that hard. I used to think it would take a fire hose to wash away a blowout. It only takes a wet wipe. It's a surprisingly quick and painless process. But I am the first to admit I might have had more experience than most with cleaning up accidents.

We've all got something that needs tending to before we start changing diapers. Maybe you need to clean up your credit report. Maybe you've been putting off your housework, but want your child to grow up in a house with bedroom doors. Me? I needed to stop shitting myself. Or, at a minimum, I needed to get better at hiding the evidence.

It's a problem that dates back to my college days at the University of Idaho.

Nearing what I thought was the end of a friend's birthday dinner during my sophomore year, I realized something had gone terribly wrong. I excused myself, and made tracks for the men's room. I was horrified. The cans must have been out of commission for a month. There were piles. TP was strung in front of the stalls like caution tape.

I was bumming a ride home with my friend Brian and thought we were wrapping things up, so I paid my bill and squeezed my cheeks together. Just then the guest of honor's parents showed up and asked for menus. They took their time. They chewed slowly. I made my way back to the stalls to see if the scene had improved. Of course it hadn't.

By the time the merriment cleared, I stepped into Brian's Bronco and told him that I didn't want to unnecessarily alarm him, but if he didn't step on it, I was going to take out his interior.

He did his best. But I didn't realize how strong-willed these things can be until that day. I wanted the momentary relief I felt to be a false alarm. But I was only kidding myself. I got through my front door too late.

Fortunately for me, my mom had just mailed me a three-pack of tighty-whities and I still had two clean pairs left. I was getting ready for summer camp in Wisconsin and had more important things to worry about than skidmarks. So, I took off the recently crisp pair of underwear and, befitting the lifestyle to which I had grown accustomed, threw them into the back of my closet.

* * *

Somewhere on the drive between Illinois and Wisconsin I got lost, a reality I didn't concede until I hit Michigan. So, I was a little weary, and maybe laying it on a bit thick when I got out of the car in front of the converted farmhouse that would be my home for the next ten weeks. On the second story, a beautiful brunette with an ear-to-ear grin and dueling pigtails was leaning against the balcony, happier to see me than any stranger I'd ever met. She'd heard what had happened on my journey and took pity on me. It would not be the last time.

I like to tell people that I met my wife at summer camp, which is true. I also like to tell them that she was a camp counselor, which is also true. I usually wait for at least one "atta boy" before I reveal that I, too, was a counselor.

Betsy had just graduated from college and was looking for something to take up the rest of her life. After a few months of long-distance phone calls at the end of the summer, she decided to make the move she'd surely dreamed of since she was a little girl: leaving her family in Illinois to move in with a chubby hipster in northern Idaho who was looking forward to a long career in the promising field of journalism.

Betsy didn't ask for much. But she did request one accommodation: a closet in which to put her clothes.

So, I tidied up. Betsy moved in. We eventually got our own place and two cats. It was bliss.

* * *

My friends love the story about the time I shit myself in Brian's Bronco. Every time there's an audience and a pitcher of beer, one of them asks me to tell it. Eventually the request was made when Betsy was at the table. I had barely hit the punch line before she put poo and poo together.

I don't remember exactly how she told her side of the story. I was busy trying to stay upright while my friends hyperventilated. The abbreviated version goes something like this: "I moved to Idaho for you. I left my family and drove two thousand miles to live with a chubby hipster I met in a barn in Wisconsin. I didn't ask anything of you. All I asked was for you to clean out a closet. You didn't. So I did. And I found a pair of shit-stained underwear and wondered whether I'd made the wrong decision. I didn't say anything because I was mortified."

She'd held it in too long. Wish I'd been so lucky.

* * *

We met when I was twenty, got married when I was twenty-two, and bought our house just after I turned twenty-four. You'd think that by the time I became a homeowner, the problem would have gone away. But one day I had an accident. I don't remember the circumstances—I'd like to think I had the flu. I'm sure it was understandable. I do remember that I hadn't worn any underwear that day. And I recall thinking: I'm just going to put these pants in the laundry bin, but I'm not going to let Betsy take them to the washing machine in the basement and discover what's been going on.

Some minutes later, I jumped out of my chair and ran to the stairs. It was too late. Just as I opened the door, she pulled my jeans off of the heap, held them up, and quietly whimpered "what?"

before she conceded to laughter. Yes, I know she loves me very much. And I love her. To show it, I've worn underwear ever since.

When she became pregnant, it was sort of like when Brad Pitt left Cate Blanchett and their baby in *The Curious Case of Benjamin Button*: he didn't want her to have to change two sets of diapers. Neither did I. Unlike Pitt, I wasn't going to leave. I wanted to make things easier for her. To do that, I was going to have to stop dropping shit around the house and start cleaning it up.

* * *

Few men have the same struggle as me, but everyone's got something that needs tending to. I've had friends give up heavy drinking, others have quit smoking. One—I'll call him Bryce here—promised his wife he'd give up porn before his baby was born.

Long self-employed and working in his home office, Bryce told me that it was easy to lose hours to the stuff. He'd promised his wife before: during their engagement, when they were talking about having kids, and, finally, when she was pregnant.

We've all got something to clean up, give up, or rethink before we have kids. It's only going to get harder after they're born. Pregnancy isn't only about getting ready for a baby, it's also about preparing for the next chapter in your life.

If that feels overwhelming, relax: you've got nine months to clean it up.

Week 5

You Don't "Need" a Bigger Place

Your baby's heart is beginning to beat.

Your lady wants to find a bigger home for the baby.

The situation: You don't disagree.

The reality: The added expense may not jive with the life you want for your family.

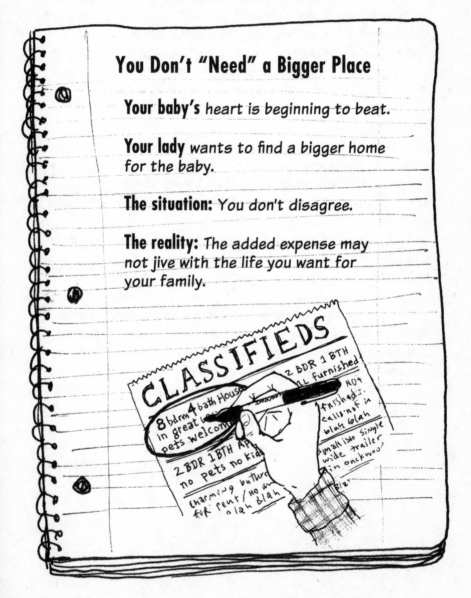

To the vast majority of our world—and throughout human history—our home would be considered large, even luxurious.

We have three bedrooms. Sure, they're small: the master doesn't have room for a king and Betsy has to walk into the baby's room to find a sweater. But they work. Well.

We have a dishwasher. Sure, it's not "installed." It has wheels and we have to hook it up to the sink to run it. Oh, and it's loud. Betsy hates that it's loud. And she doesn't think it's funny when I remind her that when she does the dishes by hand the "dishwasher" is completely silent. But, our dishes get clean. Very clean.

We have a fridge. And it even comes with a freezer! I know, I know, water's been pooling in the vegetable crisper, and that's not keeping anyone perky. And, yeah, it's been spontaneously losing power. But I figured out that if I jiggle the plug-in, the power comes back on. See, that's what was causing the puddles. The power was randomly shutting down and freezer frost was melting. It's not a problem with the fridge! It's a bad electrical outlet! The fridge works. Well.

We have a bathroom. Yes, we only have one. Sure, you have to walk through either the "master" bedroom or the baby's room to get to it. But it's healthy for babies to learn to sleep through a little noise. And Lucy sleeps. Soundly.

We have a basement! We've even fashioned an office for me and a studio for Betsy on opposite sides of the space "we" use for laundry. I know there's not much heat, but that's what space heaters are for. I can't do anything about the water that seeps in when it rains (it's Seattle, so no big deal). And if I knew what to do about the water that occasionally drips from the bathroom down to Betsy's studio, I'd be on it in a flash. But I don't. The studio still works. Thanks.

Our neighborhood also comes with a number of desirable features.

We live across the street from a park. Sure, it's an industrial park filled with old, dilapidated storage units and the three-story remains of an ancient concrete plant. Yes, it's so hazardous that the EPA recently got involved and we've been advised not to eat the blackberries on *their* side of the street. But the slumlord next door lets *tons* of blackberries grow into our backyard. We do not want for blackberries!

We live down the road from a marina. There are boats and everything. Thomas and I have a good time watching the birds and spying for fish. Yes, the vessels are a bit . . . weathered. And my old boss told me that it's the worst marina he's ever seen. And it's in foreclosure. And repeated sewage spills have made the shellfish inedible. But we can see the birds! And the mountains!

We have delightful neighbors to the west—a pair of older Jehovah's Witnesses who welcomed us to the neighborhood with some homemade hooch from which I'm still recovering. And they're so nice: they've let me borrow their weed whacker, helped me install furniture, and even donated a few pieces of wood to my fire pit. Sure, they've built a cinder-block wall on our land and are trying to steal the back few feet of our property. But they make killer booze!

None of these biographical tidbits explain why one of my high school friends proclaimed that we could never raise a family in our home. It is, she explained, just too small.

She told Betsy this at our housewarming party, years before we had kids. Apparently she had been on something of a tear that night. She sent another attendee halfway to tears by telling her the same about her house. My friend felt much worse than I did because she was already raising three children in her home. "And we're doing *just fine*!" I overheard her say in that tone of defeated defensiveness and understanding that also mildly concedes the point.

It's not only that this party pooper grew up in the biggest house among our crew. There's also a long-standing, inborn societal expectation that when you have kids, you have to get a bigger place, no matter how big your place is. HGTV has ridden this phenomenon to ratings Valhalla.

One of my favorite episodes of HGTV's *Buying and Selling* (one of the 473 shows on the network about buying and selling) is the one where the twin bro hosts try to help Jenn and JP get out of the hellhole they've been living in so they can give their only child, Benjamin, "the best life possible," according to his mother. And, in her defense, they really do live in squalor.

Their house is, unconscionably, beautiful and made of brick. It has, if you can believe it, only three bedrooms. And it's in a *quiet suburban neighborhood*! That's the real problem. They bought the house not realizing the hood was filled with old people, and there's not enough socializing for their eighteen-month-old son.

It gets worse. They put li'l Ben in the bedroom right next to the kitchen, so they refuse to use the microwave or cook dinner after he goes to sleep, for fear of waking him. Looking for a new home, Jenn puts the scenario in black and white: "If we make the wrong choice here, then Benjamin will be the most affected."

It really is an untenable situation. And we should know. I feel bad every time I get another beer at 10:30 because the door of the fridge *always* bangs into Lucy's bedroom door. This has never caused her to stir, but I can only assume that's because she's been awake whimpering herself to almost-sleep, thinking about the life she's been brought into, and wondering why her parents don't want to give her the best life possible.

Fortunately for Benjamin, his parents are actually looking out for his best interests. The brothers help his folks find a new home and sell their shit box for more money than it's worth. It's enough to drive Jenn to tears of joy. "I'm starting to give myself the chance to look into the future and to see that we're going to be able to provide for our son the way we want to. I finally get to believe in the dream. We finally get to provide the best childhood for Ben. I'm so excited!" Aren't we all.

We could all use more space. And we all want to give our children a happy home in which they can explore their interests. But "best life possible" is a mirage, perpetually out of reach. More is always possible. Better always lives around the corner. Your home is your biggest expenditure. The added expenses of a larger home could easily mean the difference between both parents working full-time and one staying home, or at least getting creative with your work situation.

I'm not suggesting that moving into a bigger place in a safer neighborhood with "better" schools is a bad idea. I'm merely suggesting that it might be possible to make having a kid work in the home that you're in now. If you think you'd be happier in a smaller house with a more flexible work environment that's closer to the life you want for your family, it might be worth penciling out.

If you just don't think it possible that you could raise your family of three in the place you're living in now, go pick up a copy of Jim Gaffigan's *Dad Is Fat*, and read about how the comedian raised a family of seven in a two-bedroom apartment in Manhattan. As my old roommate, Bill, used to say: "If *Jurassic Park* taught us anything, it's that nature finds a way."

As for us, there's really nothing we can do about our living situation at the moment. The grass in the backyard is dead. We found splattered raccoon blood on the kiddie pool yesterday. And I still haven't figured out why water drips into Betsy's art studio. Oh, and the decrepit concrete plant has been removed and I'm worried that the landlord will build some neighborhood-killing condos.

I can only hope my children will one day forgive me for not providing them with the best life possible.

Week 6

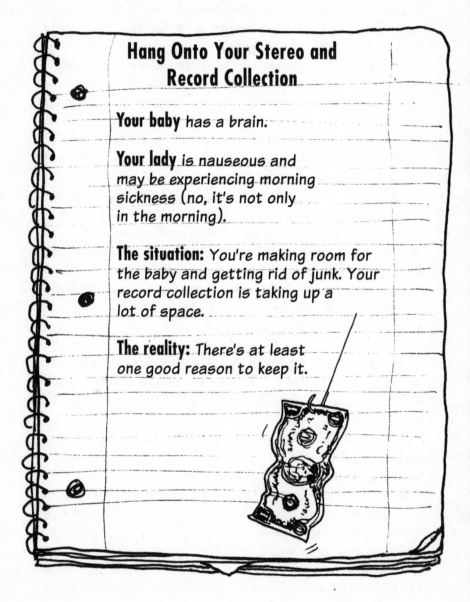

Hang Onto Your Stereo and Record Collection

Your baby has a brain.

Your lady is nauseous and may be experiencing morning sickness (no, it's not only in the morning).

The situation: You're making room for the baby and getting rid of junk. Your record collection is taking up a lot of space.

The reality: There's at least one good reason to keep it.

Although my basement office takes on water, doesn't get much heat, and boasts a window/fire escape that would make a fire marshal wince, Betsy has found it a suitable room to house overnight guests. She has also deemed it an appropriate place for Thomas to play, as long as I'm in the room. Once he reached that age when he wasn't putting curious objects in his mouth—and my office is littered with them, some of them intended to be swallowed before they'd become petrified—I felt comfortable turning my back to compose the odd e-mail or two while he puttered around. No sooner had I done this did he uncover a stash of child porn.

"Daddy! The boy's naked!" Thomas exclaimed. "He's not wearing a swimming suit!"

My office doesn't only double as our guest room. It's also the repository for the LPs, CDs, and cassettes that I've collected in life, which includes a solid decade writing about music, a career that comes with no financial security and armloads of self-doubt, but plenty of free records. Amidst the shelves of LPs and stacks of CDs, Thomas had discovered my copy of Nirvana's *Nevermind*, which, of course, features a picture of a naked infant boy in a swimming pool on the cover.

Thomas enthusiastically encouraged me to put the CD on, and as he heard "Smells Like Teen Spirit" for the first time, his eyes lit up, his smile grew, and he began to bounce. The urge to dance is a primal response. And as his body began to flail, I took him by the hands and we formed our first father-son mosh pit, which culminated with me swinging him by an arm and a leg and flinging him onto the futon.

When the song was over, he put it on again. And again. Kids love listening to songs over and over. They're like little FM radio programmers. When they find a hit, they stick with it until love for a song has turned to loathing.

There have been countless father-son mosh pits since and Thomas has moved on from "Teen Spirit" to "Breed." He has a CD player now, and he's known to skip ahead to track four and play "Breed" over and over, alone in his room, a one-man army moshing in the mirror.

I began putting my record collection together in earnest at fifteen, when I took a part-time job sweeping the floors at that lowbrow record store in Poulsbo and started bringing home records that I bought for three bucks—and some that I took in lieu of a paycheck. I was the youngest employee on staff by at least a generation, the only one who was excited to put on Jethro Tull. I didn't understand why the manager would dryly quip "your sperm's in the gutter" when I put on *Aqualung* until my ninety-ninth listen, or why you couldn't like Wings if you were into John Lennon (I still think *Band on the Run* is brilliant).

In the age of Spotify and music-streaming services—of which I am a longtime fan and subscriber—it's somewhat impractical to maintain a record collection. And for a solid two years I didn't have my stereo set up, unmotivated by the convenience of millions of songs in the cloud. To clutter our office/guest room/play room/swamp with such duplicity actually feels borderline irresponsible. And during our frequent moves, I have considered getting rid of the collection altogether. But I can't bring myself to do it. For this, I credit Thomas and I blame my mom.

When I was in high school, my mom scolded me for selling a few CDs I'd grown tired of. It wasn't a scolding, actually, as much as a reminder: "You've liked discovering the music your dad and I kept." Of course, she was right. In ways perhaps greater than she understood.

Sure, my folks' cache of LPs was my entry to Creedence, *Rubber Soul*, and Stevie Wonder. But it was also a window into who my parents are. Nothing, for example, could illuminate such a specific piece of my dad's personality and history than his copy of Simon & Garfunkel's *Parsley, Sage, Rosemary and Thyme*, which proudly features the index card from the library, which we all assume is still wondering when they'll get their recording of "Homeward Bound" back.

I'm keeping my records for the same reason I'm glad my parents did. Not only will Thomas and Lucy be turned onto some great music, they'll also have a chance to find a few of the biographical bread crumbs I've refused to tidy up. When they ask about the Doors, I'll tell them I can no longer stand the band, but I used to work at a record store owned by a man who was obsessed with Jim Morrison. If they go digging deep enough, they'll find the copy of John Coltrane's *Crescent* that my dad bought for me at Chicago's Virgin Megastore when I was in junior high ("Dad, what's a Virgin Megastore?"), or the copy of Elliott Smith's *XO* that he gave me when he dropped me off at college.

And if they develop a taste for swing, they might wonder why a guy named Harold Jones signed my copy of *Basie Straight Ahead*. And I will tell them the story about the time I took a job at a music camp in Wisconsin so I could spend a week with Count Basie's favorite drummer, and came home with the woman they call mom.

We don't all rely on our record collections to document the milestones of our life. But when you're making room for the kid, you're forgiven for not always being sensible, and holding onto a few things that can give your child a trail to your past and a good excuse to mosh.

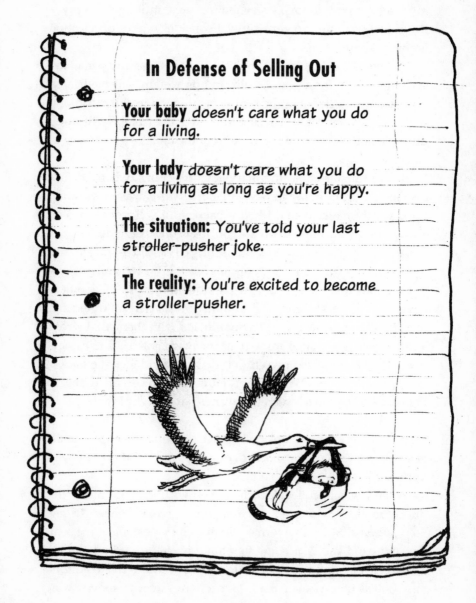

In Defense of Selling Out

Your baby *doesn't care what you do for a living.*

Your lady *doesn't care what you do for a living as long as you're happy.*

The situation: You've told your last stroller-pusher joke.

The reality: You're excited to become a stroller-pusher.

I got the call—OK, the e-mail—right after I got out of the shower. When I apply for jobs, or pitch editors stories, I check my e-mail on my iPhone every ten minutes until I get a reply— if I'm lucky enough to get a reply. I consider replies of rejection accomplishments.

I'd been applying for a lot of jobs, and checking my e-mail every ten minutes for a year. I'd also put on weight, self-medicated my anxiety, and learned the best ways to get a healthy drink on without it looking like I was getting a buzz (rotating through multiple bottles, or drinking wine from the box is a good place to start).

Before I'd started seeing marvelous rejections, when I'd first decided that continuing to work at *Seattle Weekly* wasn't working, I'd instantly realized that I had a backlog of solicitors to reject, and promptly afforded them the courtesy I was being denied.

As the music editor, I had thousands of unread e-mails in my inbox—most of them from publicists hoping I'd write about one of the bands that pays them to e-mail music editors. A few others were from writers who hoped to write for the paper. I'm terrible at writing people back, and I sympathized with them all. I wrote a few publicists, mined my e-mail for every pitch I'd left unattended, and convinced myself that karma would kick me back a response of my own. When I got out of the shower, I had one. A big one. *Rolling Stone*'s recruiter wanted to know if I would give her a call.

I told Betsy, and the look on her face felt better than the e-mail. She was excited, a little shocked, but most of all, I think she was impressed.

When I was in college and had been writing about music for fifteen minutes, I started pitching the big magazines: *Rolling Stone, Blender, SPIN*. I've tormented myself by peeking at the sent box in my old Yahoo! account to remind myself what I was up to. The really embarrassing part is the things I did to make editors take notice of my snail mail. One of my favorite moves was lighting things on fire. Seriously. I lit my business cards and the corners of my cover letter on fire thinking, This will definitely get their attention! Who else sends burned business cards!? I'm painfully sure my correspondences were noticed.

My mentor and friend Shawn, then a reporter and editor at the local paper, is the person responsible for me being a writer and making a living putting pen to paper. After a chance encounter, he hired me to write a story a week at twenty bucks a pop. In time, he became the person I asked to proof the cover letters I sent off to earth's biggest magazines. Gladly, he did his duty, which included telling me: "You realize this is like you trying to pitch for the Blue Jays, right?" I'm sure I didn't. But when I applied for a job at *Rolling Stone*, I knew I was asking to pitch for the Blue Jays, and this scout was telling me they wanted to see more of my fastball.

Betsy knew that I was a writer. She knew I was an employable writer. She also knew that working at *Rolling Stone* is as rarefied a profession as pitching for the Blue Jays, and I was being considered for a job in the bullpen. I know my wife loves me unconditionally. I know that I could put on seventy-five pounds, and she'd still stand by my considerable side. But men never stop wanting to impress their wives. If they do, there's something wrong, and you'll know they've stopped if they've added seventy-five pounds and won't stop talking about the time they almost pitched for the Blue Jays.

It wasn't only the particulars of the job that were exciting. Working at *Rolling Stone* represented an opportunity to stay in the game. I'd been at the *Weekly* for five years, and had seen one modest raise. I wasn't angry with management. I understood the fix the industry was in. But I didn't want to give it up. Our savings account was rapidly heading toward empty, and continuing my current gig no longer felt like a feasible way to feed a family.

Working at *Rolling Stone* would let me put off the larger question: was I willing to give up the profession I loved and had trained for to support my family? I'd seen plenty of friends and colleagues make the transition to full-blown adulthood by leaving journalism behind to seek professions with the stability and paychecks that responsible breadwinners bring home to their families.

Rolling Stone is and isn't what it once was. It's not the magazine that it was in the seventies, eighties, and nineties. It doesn't have the cultural force—no magazine does. But it remains the most famous pop-culture magazine in the world, and the dream job of journalism students around the country. I guess you could say my gig at *Seattle Weekly* was, too.

I wrote about music for a living in one of the best music cities in the world. I got paid to see Radiohead. I got to drink at my desk at ten in the morning. I went to summer music festivals on the clock. It was the job I'd always wanted, and the realization that my time was up, that I had to leave, was bruising. When a well-paid tax lawyer told me that I had the best job in the world I wanted to cry. I knew I had the best job in the world. It burned me up to think that I'd spent a year trying to leave it. It's surreal to realize you have your dream job; it's crushing when you realize it's time to go.

The chat interview was brief: Tell me what you've been up to? Are you open to moving to New York? How much do you make? When I told her, she gasped.

"Yeah," I said.

"How much do you want to make?"

"About double that."

"Yeah, that's about what we pay for this job."

Yes, I know it's more expensive to live in New York, but I'm on the phone with *Rolling Stone*, and they're wondering if I'm interested in a job at double my current salary. Um, yeah, I'll keep listening.

She wrapped up the chat by telling me that she'd like me to talk to the deputy managing editor. "Could you do Monday?"

At the time, we were living in White Center, the southern-most corner of what can reasonably be considered Seattle, because it was the closest to the city we could afford with two rooms and a yard. A one-bedroom apartment downtown had been perfect for just the two of us. But after Thomas was born, things got complicated.

The apartment was close enough for me to walk to a couple of nearby clubs, and it was not uncommon for me to put Thomas and Betsy to bed at ten, walk to a show, come home after two, and give Thomas a bottle. One night I returned home to find a note on our door. It said something to the effect of, "Hey! We just bought this building. We're your new landlords. In sixty days, your rent is going up 40 percent. Have a good night."

That was the push we needed to find a new place, so we went to White Center, the most ethnically diverse neighborhood in town. Cynics would say we were gentrifying the neighborhood. But, come on, we were gentrified out of our old neighborhood and moved to the only other one we could afford. Who's being gentrified now?

Monday came, and I was ready. I had poured over every recent issue of *Rolling Stone* that I could get my hands on. My Moleskine was packed with scribbled ideas and doodles of hypothetical, laid-out pages of the magazine. And the house was quiet: Betsy and Thomas took a hike while I took the call. Except I didn't take the call. "[Insert name of deputy managing editor here] is actually out ill today," Ms. Recruiter put down in an e-mail. "So we need to cancel the phone interview. How is Thursday?"

Of course, there was nothing wrong with Thursday. But, yeah, there was a complication. My in-laws were coming to town. They'd be in the house on Thursday. My in-laws are perfectly wonderful people who would be happy for me. But this would mean we'd have to let a couple more people in on the situation, and every time you tell someone else, that's another phone call you have to make when it doesn't work out. I also wasn't exactly thrilled about my in-laws seeing me at my most neurotic and alcohol dependent.

Sure enough, Thursday came, as it always does. My in-laws wished me well. Betsy wished me well. Thomas wore his footie pajamas.

I pulled the magazine's website up on my MacBook, rolled out my notes, and placed the call. I'm going to spare you the details here. I'm sure you can guess for yourself that the interview did not take place. E-mails were sent, calls were made, a cubicle was walked by. But, no, the interview did not take place. "How's Monday?" the recruiter asked.

I don't know. You tell me: how is Monday!?!? Can we work backward? How about you tell me *any time or place* for this interview to go down, and I'll be there? I'm not kidding. You tell me to go down to the airport (yes, our reasonably priced accommodations came with a view of all incoming jets) and take the next plane to New York City and I'll do it.

The best I could muster was: "Monday will work just fine. Thanks."

To my great surprise, the interview did take place on Monday. Sure, it was a half hour late, and I had to call about a dozen times, but I got the deputy managing editor on the phone. He sounded nice, gregarious, charismatic, and shocker of all shockers, he was impressed with my resume. I did most of the talking, and he punctuated my accomplishments with verbal nods of interest. After fifteen minutes, he told me that since we'd gotten started late—did "we" get started late? —he had to cut our chat short, but he wanted to pick it right back up in the afternoon.

No, we did *not* pick things back up in the afternoon. Yes, I called him (several times), but I never got through. I did get an e-mail: "Tomorrow afternoon?" Of course.

We were on the phone for ten minutes before he said he wanted me to take an editing test. I was floored. After three weeks of no movement, and apparent dodging of my calls, he was pushing down on the gas. He made the test sound easy: "Just tell me what you'd do to a couple stories." He said he'd send me the test that night.

No, no, of course he didn't send me the editing test that night, or that week. But, damn, he wanted me to take an *easy* editing test! The interview had been a cinch! I had no problem imagining that the editing test would not be the last rung of this relationship. It would just be a delayed rung.

At this point, Betsy and I were giving up any pretense of not getting our hopes up. We shopped for apartments, researched neighborhoods, enlisted a friend in Manhattan to check out a couple of blocks in Brooklyn. We learned the difference between Bushwick and Williamsburg. And I started to worry about money.

I saw apartment deposits and agent fees running into what counts as a down payment where we come from, and I didn't want anything—especially money—to stop me from taking the job and moving our family to New York. Plus, *Rolling Stone* apparently expected us to move across the country "on our own." To be sure we'd be able to cover everything, I started accepting more of the credit card offers I received in the mail. With the means, motivation, and energy to move, we waited. And waited.

These delays were not without their advantages. Every day that *Rolling Stone* put me off was another day they were not turning me down. I liked being in consideration for the job. Yeah, it was annoying to be put off. Yeah, I was a bit miffed that they couldn't get it together to send me the easy editing test. But I liked being a contender. Anticipation is often the best part of any journey, and this was an anxiety I was not anxious to be rid of: I liked wondering whether or not I was going to be asked to take a job I'd dreamed of having since I was a teenager writing stories for Shawn at twenty bucks a pop.

I think I always knew that I would never see the editing test. I wanted to believe differently. A month after I last heard from

Rolling Stone's deputy managing editor, Betsy and I were faced with a decision: extend the lease on our house in White Center, or move back into the house we owned in Bremerton (our tenants were moving out). I knew that if we went down either road, it would make a quick move to New York City nearly impossible. So I sent one final note to the deputy managing editor. Looking back, it's just embarrassing, and translucently desperate:

> *Hey, [deputy managing editor]:*
>
> *How's it going? Hope y'all had a good weekend.*
>
> *Hey, I don't want to get too personal, but like I mentioned a couple weeks ago, I'm bumping up against the deadline to make a housing decision. I'm still very interested in the position, and don't want to do anything that would make me unable to move to New York City. Do you think you could let me know whether I'm still a candidate for the job, and if you want to move forward? I totally understand that you're really busy and things come up. But if you could let me know if I'm still in the running, it would help me make arrangements on my end.*
>
> *Thanks for understanding!*
>
> *Best, Chris*

You already know that I didn't hear back from him. I sent a note to the recruiter to ask for advice. A few days later she let me know the job had been put "on hold."

Betsy and I moved back into our house in Bremerton, a tacit acknowledgement that I wouldn't be going to work for *Rolling Stone*. Two months later, the magazine announced a round of layoffs. Among those let go was an associate editor, the same position I had been applying for.

Had I been offered the job, I would have spent a lot of money—money I didn't have—to get my family to New York City. Broke, living in an expensive city with no family and few friends, and the last one through the door, I would have without question been the first one cut when layoffs hit the floor.

It's a unique feeling to be considered for the job of a lifetime. It's even more extraordinary to be grateful that you didn't get it.

But a strange thing happened while I was waiting to hear from *Rolling Stone*. My eyes began to wander.

Before Thomas was born, I never thought seriously about doing anything other than journalism. In the deep recesses of my psyche, I viewed leaving the trade—especially for money—as selling out. But when the balances on our savings and credit cards started trading places, I began, for the first time, to think seriously about ways I could support my family that did not involve writing for a newspaper.

I noticed an add on Craigslist for job openings at the first-ever Filson factory store. I'd been a fan of Filson ever since my grandpa gave me his classic Filson Cruiser jacket, and I pounced. In my cover letter, I mentioned the jacket, my years in journalism, and that "I've been considering a career change." That last part caught me off guard. I meant it. And that's what startled me.

I despise the phrase "having a baby changes everything," because it always carries the undertone of "and it sucks." The "changes everything" crowd is wrong on many fronts, but I'll concede that they were at least a little right—having Thomas

changed important things, for which I am unconditionally grateful. The realization that I could at least imagine myself doing
something else was comforting in two ways:

1. I was happy to discover that supporting my family was
   more important than my ego and my career.

2. I thought of myself at age fifty, still working as a newspaper man, and looking back at the last twenty years of
   my life thinking that I'd lived a life with blinders on,
   and it made me sad. I'd lost none of my passion for
   journalism, for telling stories, working with writers and
   collecting sources, but it was a relief to learn that it
   wasn't the most important thing in my life, and I was
   willing to explore other career options.

All that said, I still felt like a sellout, especially when I thought
about the bands that I covered who would give anything to have
a passion that comes with health insurance and doesn't require
them to be away from their families, living in broken down vans
and dirty backstage greenrooms for months at a time. I was enjoying what I was doing more than I ever had. But my trajectory
was unsustainable. And I was torn between doing what I loved,
and making a career move for the money—not just money, I understood, but a life for my family.

I once asked the great saxophonist James Moody if he ever
had a backup plan. He bristled at the question. "If you can do
something else," he said, "do it." Increasingly, it's become the
same for journalists. Some time later, I asked Branford Marsalis if
he agreed with Mr. Moody's "If you can do something else, do it"
remark. He said no: his drama teacher was still broken up that he
didn't pursue the stage. He had options. Maybe I did, too. Maybe
Filson was an option.

The factory outlet job was not for me, but Filson asked if I'd work the occasional weekend shift at their flagship store in Seattle. It wasn't a journalism gig, but it was something I was interested in and it would help pay the bills. I was in.

Everyone addresses the "sellout" moment after they become a dad. If it's not your career, then it's your lifestyle. And there's societal pressure to live life the way you did before you had kids, otherwise you're compromising. You're selling out. I think it's more accurate to say that you're evolving. Why would you want to live the rest of your life the way you did at twenty-five?

Glen Hansard, the front man of the Swell Season, once articulated his thoughts on moving forward: "At some point you need to have a bunch of kids and go live on a farm. That's the deeper song," he told the *New York Times*. "That's when the artist goes to another level. If you're a dude who's doing gigs and pulling chicks, still doing that at 55, then, dude, you haven't gone to the next place."

It's not just the artist. Moms, dads, everyone: there's wisdom, not shame, in going to the next place.

What to Expect When She's Reading *What to Expect*

Your baby is the size of a pinto bean.

Your lady is reading *What to Expect When You're Expecting.*

The situation: It's helping familiarize her with the many issues that could arise during her pregnancy.

The reality: It's also freaking her out.

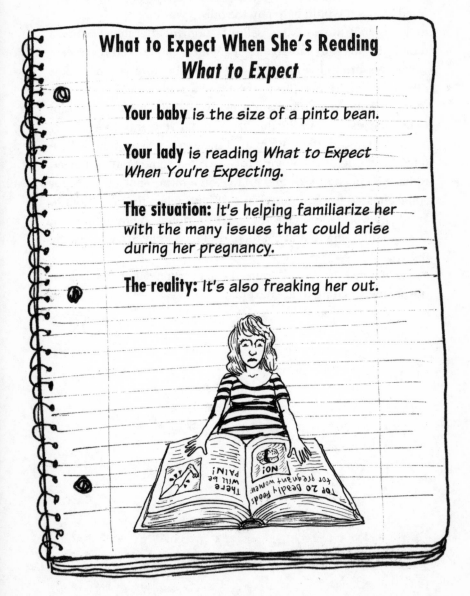

was on the phone with Ginger Zee, the *Good Morning America* meteorologist, days after she announced that she was expecting her first child, and, by way of small talk, asked her whether she was all stocked up on parenting manuals and apps. Yes, she said. In fact her husband made fun of her because she had to check in with each of her many apps every night before she went to bed.

"What I like about the apps versus the books, though, is that you get one tidbit," she told me, "versus the books where you can really wrap yourself up into this tornado spiral of doom and destruction and you think the world is ending, and I go to bed just scared out of my mind."

One of the big differences between the pregnancy landscape for women today compared to what their mothers went through is the overwhelming amount of information available to them— and forced upon them. Everyone's an armchair expert (guilty!). Everyone has advice. And the glut of information available drives up the state of anxiety during pregnancy, which is naturally an anxiety-producing time for women.

The cottage industry of websites, apps and, um, books on the topic is a double-edged sword. It's hard to argue that it's bad for women to have information about what's going on with their bodies. But some of the obstetricians I spoke to believe that the overabundance of information is intensifying the anxiety.

"It's good to prepare and think about the pregnancy, but I try to get them to think about the healthy state of pregnancy—that it's just a natural thing—instead of getting on the Internet and trying to find out all the things that could go wrong or all the things you might be doing wrong," Dr. Judy Kimelman, an obstetrician in Seattle, told me. "I think there's a really negative focus and illness sort of focus on it."

The elephant in the room here is Heidi Murkoff's *What to Expect When You're Expecting*, read by 90 percent of expectant mothers, according to the publisher. It's not a stretch to say that the popular tome has helped turn pregnancy into a panic zone. A more accurate title—and I know, I'm not one to speak about accurate titles, but stay with me—would have been *All of the Things That You Could Possibly Worry About While You're Pregnant, Because You Don't Have Enough Things to Worry About When You're Pregnant.* This is why some OBs advise against reading it.

"I recommend against it because it almost reads like: here are all the things that could go wrong in this trimester," Dr. Kimelman told me. "I think it adds a lot to anxiety."

It wasn't supposed to be this way. Murkoff wrote the book because she wanted women to sleep better at night. But it's had the opposite effect. Its success helped launch an industry of overworry and alarmism.

"*What To Expect* is, then, finally, a self-fulfilling prophesy," Allison Benedikt wrote on *Slate*, "because what to expect as an expectant mother today is to be bombarded with information about how you are doing it wrong—whether it is carrying a baby in your womb, pushing it out, or raising it."

But, the fact remains, your lady is probably reading it. And you should expect to hear a number of questions about whether she should call the doctor because she's feeling a miscarriage coming on. I know that sounds glib, but it's important to fight the urge to dismiss her worries.

Dr. Kimelman said one of the best things men can do is help their ladies understand that their anxiety is normal and hormonal, and to help her be rational.

And if she's reading *What to Expect*, make sure that she's reading the most recent version—and if she's got a hand-me-down copy, she just might not be. The earlier printings have even more strict dietary restrictions, among other things, and make some assertions that experts have long since dismissed.

For example, performing oral sex on a pregnant woman will *not* create an embolism that could kill mother and baby—but it can help relieve stress. This is information you'll appreciate having almost as much as she will.

Week 9

Ask Her What You Can Be Doing Better

Your baby is starting to look like a human being.

Your lady seems upset.

The situation: She is upset.

The reality: She's not showing much, if at all, so it's easy to casually forget that she's pregnant. You and I have both been a bit lazy.

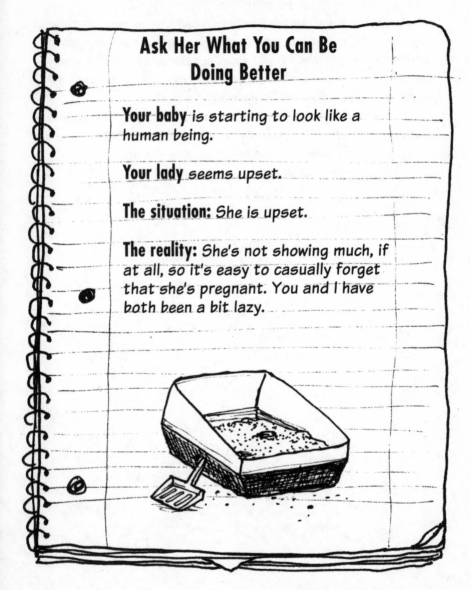

Your heart's in the right place: you want to do everything possible to make pregnancy a little bit easier for your lady. You want to be there. You're gonna go to class and you've volunteered to pretend to read this book. But there is a shortcut to making her feel better: ask her what you can be doing better. I had a humbling moment while Betsy was pregnant with Lucy, when I asked her to write down what I could be doing better. Here's what she said:

- Compliment me every day. I know you usually do, but I do remember on the days you forget.
- Do the cat pan every day without me nagging you. Or, if it stinks—twice in one day.
- Read the parenting books I read.
- Make dinner on the nights I work all day.
- Massage me without a pretext of sex required/insinuated.
- Offer/Ask if there are things I need help with to get ready for the baby. Often.

During the first trimester, when women aren't showing very much, it's easy for men to forget that they're growing a baby, and that everything they do becomes harder. This difficulty increases throughout the pregnancy. Pregnancy lasts a long time. She doesn't get used to it. It doesn't get easier. We can get distracted from it, but she can't.

When Lucy was about six months old, I mentioned to Betsy that, you know, I couldn't believe how fast she was growing, and that I could hardly remember her being pregnant. This comment stopped her in her tracks. It was both untrue—I certainly remember her being pregnant, I was just . . . yeah, it came out way wrong—and illuminating.

I'd spent so much of her pregnancy thinking about the next step—thinking about how to make things work when Lucy was born, when we'd have two kids to feed—that I hadn't always been as attentive to the things she needed *right now*, as the afore-mentioned list can attest. Yes, all the things I had to do were im-portant. All the conversations I was having with myself, all the scenarios I was exploring were necessary. But she was going through the same thing. She was thinking about our next steps, too. But she could never escape the reality that she was carrying one child while raising another.

I'd like to say that I pinned the list of shortcomings up in front of my computer and made sure I checked them off every day. But I didn't.

Looking at Betsy's list again, the last item feels the most damn-ing: "Ask if there are things I need help with to get ready for the baby. Often . . . "

The message is clear: don't just ask once what you can be do-ing better. Ask every day.

week 10

Respect Yourself: Don't Carry a Diaper Bag

Your baby has officially graduated from embryo to fetus.

Your lady has a uterus the size of a grapefruit.

The situation: You're putting together a fatherhood shopping list.

The reality: You've already got a lot of the tools you're going to need. But treat yourself to a nice bag.

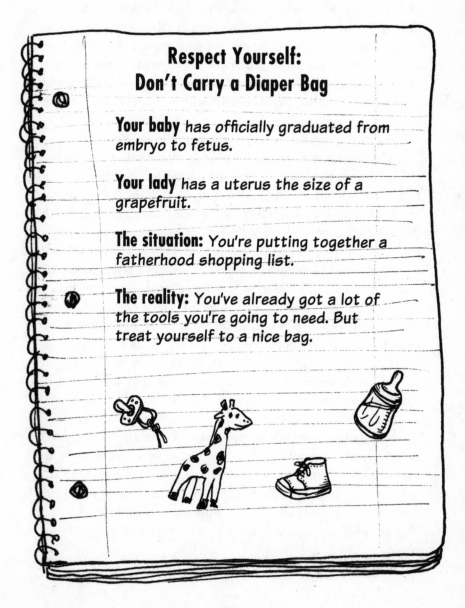

got into journalism for the money. I was eighteen, broke, and looking for a paycheck. Sitting in my dorm room at the end of the first semester of my freshman year, I was out of what little money I'd saved from my summer gig at Old Navy (which had been fabulous). I didn't need much. Meals, rent, and tuition were taken care of by my loving, successful, and generous parents. But I needed something. I looked around for campus jobs online, and there was a note about writing articles for the student newspaper, the *Argonaut*.

I was a little pinched when it came to experience. I had recently created a website (today, people would call it a blog, but this is 2000 we're talking about), and written a couple items about music. They both may have been about Jackson 5 reunion rumors. Oh, and for my high-school senior project, I shadowed a deejay at KJR, one of Seattle's classic-rock stations. The internship was informative in several ways. To start, I learned that the entire "archive" that KJR pulled from was a rack of CDs that fit on the studio wall. I was also informed by my internship supervisor that being a DJ doesn't take a college degree; you can have done anything, even been a flight attendant, which this guy didn't make sound so bad. Stewardesses, he told me, like to fuck.

The *Argonaut* kids were, I'm not going to say *impressed* with my "radio experience," as they called it, but they mentioned it. And they hired me, more or less, on the spot.

I didn't take AP English in high school—or any other AP class, for that matter. I was never encouraged to pursue writing. So, I didn't get into journalism because I had a long love affair with the printed word or defending the truth. I'm not ashamed to admit that I got into journalism for the eleven bucks a story the *Argonaut* paid me. But I loved every single minute of it.

I got into Filson for the money, too. I loved every second of it, too.

Like working in radio, working at Filson was educational and illuminating in ways I didn't see coming. To start, there were the hookers.

I don't think I've led a completely sheltered life. But I don't have any firsthand experience with prostitutes. Yeah, I used to see women and their pimps come into the *Weekly* office on Tuesday afternoons to pay cash for their color ads in the back of the paper. But it still seemed removed. I never connected the dots that my paycheck was, in part, funded by women who sold their services and men who paid for them.

When I worked the 9 a.m. shift at Filson on Saturday mornings, I left my house in Bremerton at 6:45, walked to a ferry, and sailed across the Puget Sound for an hour before strolling through Seattle's Pioneer Square neighborhood when it still smelled like the night before. A few lost boys were usually finding their way home and Cowgirls Inc. always looked like it needed a shower. The only other working men I would see were construction workers—dads who, like me, were working Saturdays for a few extra bucks—headed to one of the many towers of condos the city has been growing.

One morning the boys and I were making our way to our respective job sites when a stretch limousine pulled up between the condo and my path to work. A man in a tuxedo stepped out, held the hand of a woman in a tutu, and escorted her and two friends to their car in the parking lot. This was truly the morning after. All of us kept walking, then I heard the hollers from the construction workers. I turned to see that one of the women had lit a cigarette, removed her top, and drove away topless. It was a working morning for us all.

Filson specializes in work-wear and gear for men who play seasonal sports: hunting, fishing, etc. But the experience of working at Filson was distinguished by spectator sports. Because the store was nuzzled behind the city's baseball and football fields, our work experience was shaped by fans of the game.

I got bitter during baseball season when I saw dads taking their sons to the game on Sunday afternoons. I had a four-hour commute to work a five-hour shift. It wasn't as if Thomas got to see me much during the week. And I got jealous of the dads who weren't working two jobs and still coming up short.

Football season was a different matter. The fans didn't inspire the same kind of lifestyle envy.

The popular impression of Seattle is that it's a hyperliterate, sophisticated, tech-savvy, open-minded city. And it is. And it isn't. If you'd visited the alley behind Filson's old flagship store (RIP) before a Seahawks game you'd have seen what I'm talking about.

Public defecation and rampant intoxication didn't bother us until they started stealing the traffic cones from our parking lot. One afternoon, one of my equally bearded coworkers hand-rolled a couple cigarettes for us and we stepped out back to witness the debauchery. No sooner had we lit up did a blue-faced man motion our way and alert his friends: "Hey, look! Those two hipsters just got done fucking in there!" Go Hawks.

My backpack started falling apart not long after I took the job, and I ended up carrying my lunch to work in a paper grocery bag. I had been putting off purchasing one of the store's bags because, even with my discount, it would cost me at least a day or two's wages. Eventually, I couldn't take it anymore, and broke down and bought a Medium Field Bag, the finest accessory I've ever owned.

* * *

You know how in college people talked about keeping a "booty bag" at the ready, always packed with a Barry White CD, condoms, and a change of clothes, just in case the situation arose that you needed to head out for some sex on the quick? I know nobody ever had those bags and those situations never came up, but it was at least talked about. A diaper bag is the same thing, except that you're going to actually use it.

If you keep your bag ready at all times, it makes getting out of the house and having a life and maintaining sanity that much easier. Don't do it only for yourself: your child will get sick of the inside of the house, too. I think it's also a good idea for you and your lady to have separate bags, for a variety of reasons. First, you want to make sure the bag is always stocked with essentials, and if you're sharing the bag, you're never going to be completely sure what's left inside. Also—and I know I'm going out on a limb here—I'm assuming you have a slightly different style than your lady. You should each have a bag that you like, that makes each of you feel like a member of the human race.

Diaper bags are all ugly. They are to bags what mom jeans are to pants. Yes, they're convenient. But so are fanny packs. Just because you're a dad doesn't mean you have to submit yourself to the caricature. Get something that you like, and treat yourself if you can. When it comes to the items that you're going to be using day in and day out—car seats, high chairs, strollers, diaper bags—going cheap is going to get expensive and will eventually hold you back. This, it turns out, is one of the many lessons I learned at my new job at Filson. One day I was talking to new parents about our luggage and it dawned on me to inform them: um, yeah, this is technically called a Medium Field Bag, but it's also the best diaper bag you could ever buy. Sold.

Diaper Bag Essentials

Peanuts. No, these aren't for your baby—peanuts are a choking hazard. These are for you. Bad things happen when dads get hungry. This is a trick passed down from my favorite drummer

(see Week 6). Fill your belly first, or you won't be in a good place to fill hers. Eat when you're hungry—not when the baby is. When you get sick of peanuts, move on to trail mix, beef jerky, and high-quality meat sticks.

Wipes. Yes, these are technically for the baby, but you'll be surprised how handy these things are for the whole family. Once you introduce them into your life, you'll find all kinds of uses for them.

Diapers. Always keep at least four. As I've said before, changing a diaper really isn't a big deal, but things happen when you change diapers. Like, babies decide that as you're putting on a fresh diaper that's their cue to poo. So, don't be surprised if it takes two or three diapers to get a clean one on.

Burp rags. Don't let them pile up in your bag. When a rag starts to stiffen, you know you've left it inside for too long.

A change of clothes. One set should do fine. And if you're self-conscious about the occasional smear of snot or upchuck on your shirt, it wouldn't be a bad idea to keep a tee of your own inside just in case.

Whatever the baby's eating. As a rule of thumb, you should keep at least one meal/snack more than you think the outing necessitates. There are few things worse than having a hungry baby and no food (see: peanuts).

week 11

Safe Sex Is Great Sex

Your baby will not be hurt by your penis.

Your lady could get hurt if you're not gentle.

The situation: Pregnancy sex is like nonpregnancy sex—don't do what feels bad.

The reality: Yes, that means it can still be great.

At this point during pregnancy, if you're frustrated by the lack of sex that's taking place in your side of the duplex, let me make a suggestion: clean the bathroom and vacuum the living room.

There's conflicting research about whether men who do more chores have more sex, but all of the women I've asked about this over the last year—some of them doctors, some of them rock and rollers, some of them interior designers who live in homes strikingly similar to my own—have said that pregnant women have more energy for sex if they're not spending it all on chores.

Once you get your clothes off, there are a few sex things that are different during (and after) pregnancy.

Since I'm not a sex expert (I have witnesses), I consulted with someone who is. Dr. Roger Libby has made a career out of doling out advice on how to love one another (and yourself). In addition to counseling couples in my neighborhood, he masterminded the classic *The Better Sex Video Series* that you once saw on VHS as a kid when you couldn't get your hands on proper porn. Here are his tips and advice for sex during pregnancy, after the birth, and in the years that follow.

Be careful. "If something hurts," he says, "you don't keep doing it. That doesn't mean you can't do anything. It just means you have to experiment a little bit."

Stick with doggy style. Libby says it's a good position because you won't be putting any weight on the fetus. During the first trimester, he says, the missionary position is probably fine (as long as nobody's in pain), but later on, he recommends couples stick with doggy style or scissors side-by-side intercourse. "If you are comfortable putting female above," he says, "you can try it, but people vary on that."

Be patient: Some women are more into sex during different trimesters (mainly the second, when they often have a bit more energy), but other women, the doc says, just don't have an interest in sex at all during pregnancy. "And that's OK," he says, "you can just kiss each other and be affectionate in other ways. The man has to be very patient and loving toward his wife because she's going through some significant changes in her body that affect her emotionally and mentally." After the birth, if the woman is breast-feeding, Libby says hormonal changes can reduce a woman's libido, too. So, again, be patient.

Remember, she can be a mother and a lover. Libby says that some men have a hard time having sex with their partners after birth because they view them as mothers, not lovers. In rare instances, men never get over it. In those cases, seek help. Otherwise, get over yourself.

Wait four to six weeks after birth. That's a rule of thumb. But the doc says it's definitely something for you/her to bring up at the follow-up doctor's appointments. Some women need more time to recover after pregnancy. Her doctor will be able to give her the high sign.

Try lube. During pregnancy, Dr. Libby says because she's deficient in estrogen, it may be harder for her to lubricate. After pregnancy, she's likely to have similar issues. The doc recommends water-soluble and silicone-based lubricants rather than oil-based products.

Try foreplay. Since it's going to take longer for her to lubricate, the doc advises you to slow down.

Oral sex is fine for both of you. "My line is it's all but replaced the goodnight kiss, it's just hard to do on the doorstep." Enough said.

Don't wait until night. "The biggest mistake not just people with children, but anybody, make is waiting until late at night to have sex," Libby says. "That's when you're tired out." This is especially true in the months after birth. Get it on when you've got the energy. Make it a priority. Libby recommends couples get together for lunch. "I call it the home delivery," he says. "That's something that can be fun because it's something you anticipate and desire."

Masturbate. "During a pregnancy and soon after the birth, a guy can masturbate and so can she," he says. "That could take off a little of the pressure to be highly sexual with each other all the time. I think you need a balance between self-pleasuring and making love with each other. And I think that's a healthy thing. As Woody Allen once said: 'Don't knock masturbation. It's sex with someone I love.'"

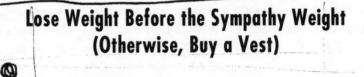

Lose Weight Before the Sympathy Weight (Otherwise, Buy a Vest)

Your baby is putting on weight—he's up to a half ounce!

Your lady is beginning to get over her morning sickness.

The situation: You heard a guy mention sympathy weight. You scoff.

The reality: If you're anything like me, you're gonna put on a lot more than half an ounce every day you're in the hospital alone. Sympathy weight is real.

The prebirth hospital tour is a pregnancy rite of passage that I don't suggest you miss. When you're driving your lady and almost-born to the hospital, you're not going to want to leave anything to chance. It's a good idea to know *in advance* where you can park (you could be there for a couple days), where to check in, what to bring, and, yes, what to order off the menu.

When Betsy and I took the tour before Thomas was born, a good-natured couple on the tour enthusiastically told us that they'd heard that the kitchen's milkshakes and chocolate cake were killer. These tips are good things to know. Hospital food has come a long way since we were born, but, like I said, there's no reason to leave important topics like this to chance. The happy couple was right: the milkshakes and chocolate cake at Swedish Hospital in Seattle are dynamite.

The thing about dining in the hospital is that the mothers eat for "free" but the fathers don't. Don't get me started on this one. It costs thousands of dollars to give birth in a hospital. Charging men six dollars for a ham and cheese omelet seems about as petty as charging extra for a couch cushion. At any rate, during the day(s) you spend in the hospital, "am I eating right?" is going to be one of the last things on your mind.

Not that it's ever at the top of my mind. But at the time, I was as svelte as I'd been in years. But right now, I look like I've been subsisting on milkshakes and chocolate cake for the last five years. Sympathy weight is real (and I've been very sympathetic). When your lady loses weight after pregnancy, it is deposited directly onto your ass. To deal with this, I believe you have two options:

1. **Hit the gym.** Children don't come with a spare tire. We provide that ourselves. If you're the kind of person who needs to go to the gym, who likes going to the gym,

who feels better going to the gym, then keep going to the gym, even if you don't think you can spare the time. Many gyms—such as our neighborhood Y—will watch your baby while you do whatever it is that people who go to the gym do when they go to the gym. Don't use your baby as an excuse for falling out of shape. I'll be the first to admit that it may be a contributing factor in my case, but it's not like I was short of excuses when I wasn't a dad.

2. **Get a vest (or two).** When I worked at Filson, my midsection went through a number of . . . incarnations. As a result, I've got their classic wool vest in size 46, 44, and 42. At one point or another, each of them has fit me perfectly. I've also come close to getting rid of the 46 and I've wondered why I still have that 42. But I'm glad I've got them all. On my worst "days" the 46 fits perfectly and the 42 acts as a girdle.

Week 13

Fight for the Fatherhood You Want for Your Family

Your baby is the size of a peach.

Your lady has tender breasts.

The situation: You're trying to figure out how you're going to get the work/life/sex balance right.

The reality: You have more options than your parents and grandparents did. Figure out what you want for your family and demand it.

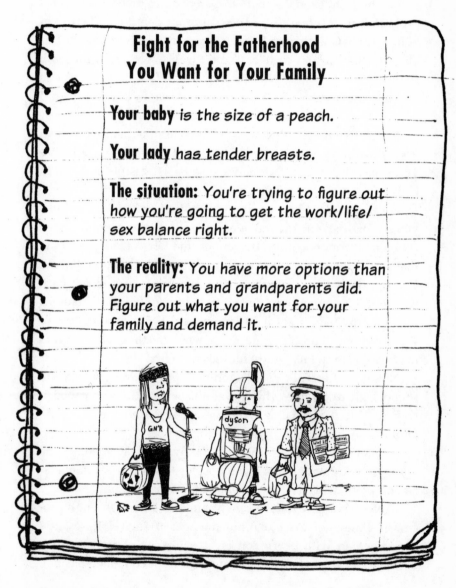

For Thomas's second birthday he got a green "computer" that quickly became his favorite toy. One of its marquee functions is the ability to send "e-mail" to parents and loved ones. Betsy programmed it while I was away at work one day. When I got home, Thomas announced that he had an e-mail for me. "Dear Daddy," the machine recited, "I can't wait to see you. I love you so much!"

I felt like a sailor who'd been gone at sea. In a way, I guess I had.

It took two hours to get to work, a commute that involved an hour on a ferry each way. This meant I left the house before Thomas woke up and returned just as Betsy was putting him to bed.

For new dads, a long commute is full of conflict. You feel like you're missing out on moments at home—the questions, the spontaneous monologues, the smiles, the hugs—and you know that you've left your partner or daycare provider holding the bag. The upside is that, well, you have two hours to yourself each way. I didn't commute by car, so if a bottle of bourbon made its way into my bag, it got light before I got home. And because I was drinking bourbon while Betsy was wrestling Thomas into his *Cars* pajamas, I felt guilty for the entire first sip.

Not long after Thomas's "computer" put me in my place, my friend Duff asked me why it was that every time he called it sounded like I was being overworked. It wasn't the first time Duff had looked out for my well-being.

After a madman tore through Sandy Hook Elementary, he wrote me—knowing I had a young son—to see if I was doing alright. When I had a cold he recommended the Neti pot.

Duff knows how to take care of himself, largely through process of elimination. As a founding member of Guns N' Roses, he's experimented with every conceivable way to abuse his body. Duff once drank his own throw up because it contained alcohol.

He underwent sinus surgery to make up for years spent snorting coke before his morning coffee. When Duff McKagan suggests I put something up my nose, I assume it's gonna be great.

Duff was right to be concerned. I was tired (all new parents are). I was overworked (all newspaper journalists are). I was underfunded (all newspaper journalists are). I didn't want to give up on newspapers, and the extra money at Filson—what I wasn't putting back into the store, of course—was helping, but my trajectory didn't seem sustainable. It was time to make a change. Soon enough, it was made for me.

Seattle Weekly was sold and an outsider was brought in to run the newsroom. A few weeks later, he requested a private meeting.

It didn't take long. He explained that he was eliminating my position and terminating my employment. I live in the newspaper business, where layoffs and restructuring are de rigueur. It'd happened to friends. It'd happened to colleagues. Still, I didn't see this one coming. The editor was obviously shaken and appeared to be fighting back tears. I stopped him. "Guys," I said, "It's OK. I'm gonna go."

He handed me a white sheet of paper that explained the details of my severance: a week's salary for every two years of service. After more than six years at the paper, I was given three weeks' pay and asked to leave the building immediately.

I grabbed my bag, quickly told friends that it was my last day, and walked out the door.

I didn't want to tell Betsy over the phone, so I called my dad as I made my way back toward the ferry. When I started to explain that I'd been fired, speaking the words out loud shocked me, and I started to cry, treating the early drinkers in the neighborhood to the sight of a chubby hipster blubbering behind his red Wayfarers.

I took my usual seat outside on the back of the boat. The sun was hot and made me sweat until the ferry turned and I shivered

in the shade. I had a clear view of Mount Rainier, the Space Needle, downtown Seattle, and the Cascade Mountains. I started
thinking about Montana.

There is a vision—an amalgam of memories—that I've visited
over the last ten years when I've been in need of reprieve. I'm
staring across the dashboard as the sun begins its descent. The
hills are brown, and the blue Montana sky runs for what has to be
forever. I'm that familiar temperature that can only be achieved
on a cross-country road trip without air conditioning, when the
breeze of a rolled-down window mellows a hint of stick on my
skin. I'm tired, but not sleepy. It's not exhausting to drive for days
at a time. It's liberating.

I drove across Montana a couple times in the years leading up
to and after graduating from college—the summer job where I
met Betsy, the trip to Wisconsin where I married her. Each of the
journeys had defined destinations with transitional underpin-
nings. I had my coordinates, but I didn't know where I was going. Because of these trips, I will forever associate the vision of
crossing "Big Sky Country" with the unbridled feeling of freedom in the unknown.

When I've called on the image in the past, a pang of longing
and a shameful tinge of regret accompany it. I'm nostalgic for a
time when the future wasn't prescribed. With a wife, child, and
career, it felt like that part of my life was over, and that I'd never
again drive into the sunset, into the bliss of the unknown.

That morning on the back of the boat, a father and husband
cut off from a way of supporting his family, I felt that unique
breed of excitement that I've only felt when I didn't know where
I was going.

To my surprise, I quickly found new ways to draw a paycheck putting pen to paper. The day after I was laid off, I learned about a copywriting gig in Filson's corporate office. They put me on a contract. Soon after, I was given my first freelance assignment for the *Wall Street Journal*. I wasn't working as a newspaper editor anymore, but I was figuring out how to make a living as a writer, doing the thing I loved.

Some months later, I interviewed James Dyson, the billionaire vacuum cleaner guy, who told me a story about pursuing an atypical career after college that resonated with my circumstances.

"I wasn't going to be a lawyer or an accountant or something sensible," he said. "I was going to go off to be an inventor and a designer, someone who created his own things. In those days, you either became an engineer and went to work for an engineering company or you were a designer. I made the decision to be an engineer, designer, and a scientist and to work on my own."

This career trajectory came with incredible risk. To manufacture his invention, Dyson borrowed a million dollars from the bank. Had he failed, he would have gone bankrupt. This, surprisingly, didn't bother his wife. "My wife had been to art school as well. So she absolutely understood the need to pursue the project, the big project."

But, I wondered: how did he rationalize such a risk?

"It was very hard. We had very little money. We used to grow our own vegetables."

But . . .

"I could make furniture. I had been taught to do it at art school. We always knew that if the idea failed, I could be a carpenter and make furniture for people. She could sell paintings. I suppose apart from the terrifying debt, failure—total failure—wouldn't be too bad. We would lose the house, and so on, but we had practical skills from which we could earn money."

I don't know how to make furniture, but I understood his point: even if my "big project" failed, I had other skills with which I could make money, something that was confirmed when I found paychecks after I was laid off. The story also felt like a challenge. I didn't have a "big project," but I wanted to be bold, to be willing to risk everything.

After my copywriting contract ended, the big project started to come into focus. Betsy was working mornings at the local community college, and could drop Thomas off at daycare on the way to work and pick him up on the way home. I made breakfast, got them out the door, and retreated to my basement office, drawing unemployment while I built up a freelance business. Things were tight, but not without their advantages.

I liked being at home to see Thomas and Betsy off in the morning. I liked being there when they got back in the afternoon. I liked teaching Thomas how to take the city bus. I liked bringing cupcakes to school at 11 a.m. on his birthday. I liked spending days with my family rather than just my evenings. I liked having sex in the middle of the day.

Nights were tough. It was harder to push back the possibility of financial calamity. I spent many sleepless nights reciting the same prayer: God, please give me the wisdom to see the path that you've laid out before me, and give me the courage to follow it.

Days were good. I was staying busy. I was still applying for jobs, but I was more interested in figuring out how I could make a living writing and editing from home. Slowly, things started to fall into place.

Duff asked me to coauthor his next book. I became a regular contributor for the *Wall Street Journal*. I wrote cover stories and features for *LA Weekly* and the *Village Voice* and found consistent work with the *Seattle Times*. Former colleagues turned up at magazines I'd never heard of and wondered whether I was in the market for freelance work. I was off unemployment and we were paying the bills. Barely. But they were paid.

One day Betsy asked me what I was thinking: what was the job I thought would be best for me and our family? I told her I didn't want a typical newspaper career or a two-hour commute anymore. I wanted to write and coauthor books, pick up stories for the *Wall Street Journal*, and write magazine articles. I wanted to work from home, to be there when Thomas went to school and woke up from his afternoon nap. I told Betsy I wanted to make her breakfast in the morning and make love after lunch.

"You know," she said, "that's pretty much what you're doing right now."

My big project, it turned out, wasn't a career as much as a lifestyle I wanted to lead with my family. With a clear idea of what I wanted, all that was left to do was to fight for it. A few months later, I saw firsthand how a couple of dads were getting it done.

* * *

When I was in college, I got to know a couple named Gerardo and Patty. They started selling tamales at the farmer's market in Moscow, Idaho, while he was a nontraditional student and she worked as a sanitation worker. She was sick of working as a janitor, and they decided it was put up or shut up time: risk it all and start the business they'd dreamed of or maintain the status quo. They went with the former, and opened Patty's Mexican Kitchen in a shack just off campus.

Through the years it grew incrementally—more tables, an expanded menu, the introduction of beer. On my last trip to Moscow, I made a point of visiting the restaurant. I hardly recognized it. What had once been little more than a taco truck without wheels had become a large, bustling outdoor restaurant.

I had a drink with Gerardo and overheard a customer ask him when they were shutting down for the winter. Huh? Sometime in the ten years I'd been away from town, they'd decided to close the restaurant from October 30 through February every year.

"Gerardo!" I said. "How the hell can you close down for four months!? And during the school year, no less!" Gerardo chuckled and told me his story.

I knew he and Patty had a son—in elementary school by the time I left town—but what I didn't know is that a few years after I left, they had another child. They couldn't run the restaurant and raise an infant, so when their newborn son was six months old, they sent him to live with Patty's mother in Nevada. "I know," he told me. "We were the worst parents ever. We never saw our kid." Worse, he didn't know they were his parents. He called his grandma "Mom."

But, why didn't you just hire a manager? "We did at first," Gerardo said, "But business slowed down. People started telling us that they'd stopped showing up when we weren't there."

A few years later, Patty got pregnant again. They had another son and for two years, he lived with Patty's mother, too. They saw the boys as often as they could, but they were more like a distant aunt and uncle than parents.

Winters were always tough for the restaurant. Sure, school was in session and there were more people in town than any other time of year, but they had become an outdoor restaurant. In the Idaho snow, business slowed to a crawl.

They decided to go nuclear. They put it all on the line once again: they closed the restaurant for four months each year to be full-time parents to their second round of kids. They took the train, went on road trips, and went to the mall and drank hot chocolate—things they couldn't do when they were working all day, every day.

I was inspired. Gerardo and I were in the same place: we both knew what our big projects were, we knew how we wanted to support our families, and we knew what kind of fathers we wanted to be. Here he was fighting for it.

Gerardo is a smart businessman, and told me the story behind a sly grin.

"Gerardo," I said, "Let me ask: do you sell more burritos in eight months than you did in twelve?"

"Of course!" he said. "It's the novelty of opening your business for the first time, only we get to do it every year. I didn't realize that until the first time we went to reopen. We had lines clear out to the sidewalk."

Last question: "Why October 30? Why not just the end of October?"

Gerardo: "Patty wanted to take the kids trick-or-treating."

Later, Gerardo explained that their oldest son grew up at the restaurant, and he hated it. But through the years he warmed back up to the place, and offered his dad free advice. Now his son's the manager and expecting his first child. Gerardo's going to keep him employed during the off-season—working catering gigs and making changes to their restaurant. But he's also going to make sure his son has plenty of time to be with his young family in the four months their restaurant is closed.

"I don't want him to make the same mistakes I made."

* * *

Some time after my trip to Moscow, I talked David Ritz into meeting me for lunch. Ritz is a prolific writer who's known for ghostwriting the memoirs of rockers like Willie Nelson, Aretha Franklin, and Aerosmith's Joe Perry. When we sat down for bacon and eggs, I told him about my situation and he nodded knowingly in his understated, tattooed, septuagenarian way. When he was my age and had his first kid, he told me, he made a career pivot, too.

He owned his own ad agency when his first child was born and decided he couldn't work a nine-to-five anymore. So he started a lengthy process of convincing Ray Charles to let him coauthor his memoir. It took some doing, but once he hooked the

Genius, the rest was history. He's become one of the most successful ghostwriters alive.

Becoming a father had been his professional making. By changing careers to be able to spend more time with his daughter, he launched a career that was far more fulfilling than the one he'd been in before.

* * *

Matt Berninger, the front man of the National, once told me that "everybody in the band realizes that there are things that are more important [than the band]. And having kids and family and stuff *around* the band is not healthy, so we schedule the band around that stuff."

I thought it noble because it felt like he was willing to sacrifice his career for his family—and he was. But what had never occurred to me is that by fighting for the life that you want for your family and putting those goals first, you can have a more fulfilling professional life as well.

I'd rather work from home and write articles and books than be an associate editor at *Rolling Stone* or the music editor at *Seattle Weekly*. But I never would have known that if I hadn't been laid off and forced to make a change and get a look at professional opportunities I'd never considered.

It's not just taco vendors and self-employed journalists who can get creative. All of us have opportunities for creative work-life scenarios that our fathers never had.

* * *

My grandfather was born on the family homestead in Montana. His father paid a doctor fifty dollars to perform the service. He later spent thirty years working as a typesetter at a local newspaper to support a family with nine kids. Men today aren't spending thirty years in the same job—and they certainly can't support an eleven-piece family as a newspaper typesetter (the job doesn't even exist at newspapers anymore).

When my dad was my age, his boss rang a bell at the beginning and end of fifteen-minute breaks. There was no telecommuting. There was no consideration of work-life balance.

Working remotely gets easier with each iPhone release and broadband upgrade; the Affordable Care Act untethered reasonably priced health insurance from permanent employment; the paternity-leave stigma is starting to wear down. There's never been a better time to get creative.

If your employer doesn't offer the kind of flexibility you're looking for, ask for it. Negotiate. Don't wait for your boss to think up new programs. Make your case.

If your bosses push back, reassure them by explaining that you'll sell more burritos in eight months than you ever did in twelve.

If they still won't budge, it might be time to learn how to build furniture.

week 14

Watch Out for Depression

Your baby *weighs about an ounce and a half.*

Your lady *seems happy and healthy.*

The situation: *Hopefully it will stay that way.*

The reality: *You need to keep an eye out for anxiety and depression—before and after the baby's born.*

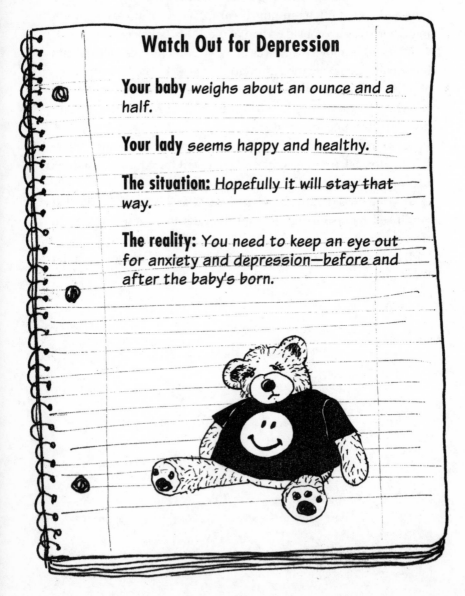

It goes without saying that your lady is going through some difficult emotional times and mood swings. Without getting into the
hormonal weeds, let's just say that she's going through uncomfortable changes that make puberty seem like a long weekend in the
same pair of underwear. But there's a difference between agitation
and frustration during pregnancy and straight-up depression.
Many women get—and get over—the "baby blues" in the two
weeks after birth. Depression is a different animal.

Somewhere between 14 and 23 percent of women get depressed during pregnancy, and between 8 and 19 percent report frequent depressive symptoms after birth. On the mild
end, depression can turn what should be some of the most joyous days of life into a time of fear and anxiety; on the darker
end, it can cause women to do extremely harmful things to
themselves and their babies. And it can occur even a couple
years after birth.

To get a primer on what men can do to help, I spoke to Sonia
Murdock, the cofounder and executive director of the Postpartum Resource Center of New York. Here's what she said:

Watch for these symptoms during pregnancy:

- She doesn't appear like her everyday self
- She doesn't seem as happy
- She seems more irritable, down, and overwhelmed
- There are changes with eating—such as eating too much
  or eating too little
- There are changes with sleeping—such as sleeping too
  much and sleeping too little
- She's not interested in things that she used to enjoy
- She displays symptoms of obsessive compulsive disorder

When I suggested to Murdock that some of these symptoms—doesn't appear like herself, changes in eating/sleeping,

irritability—describes every single pregnant woman I've met, she says to put it on a range: Is it mild, moderate, or severe? Is it impeding her daily function? Has she stopped taking care of herself? Is she not herself? That's when it's time to speak up.

Watch for these symptoms after pregnancy:

- She has trouble sleeping while the baby sleeps
- She feels numb or disconnected from the baby
- She has scary or negative thoughts about the baby
- She worries that she will hurt the baby
- She feels guilty about not being a good mom, or ashamed that she cannot care for the baby

Murdock says the latter is particularly acute among women who are used to being in control and put together. "A lot of women will express that they feel that they're becoming a burden, that 'my husband doesn't need somebody who is going through this. He needs somebody who has it all together. I was that woman before, but now I just feel very overwhelmed.'"

Murdock recommends the following:

Remind her that it's not her, it's the illness. "It's not them," Murdock says. "It is treatable, and it's very important to reach out and get the help that they need."

You need to speak up at the doctor's office, too. Murdock says that many women are embarrassed to talk about mental health issues, so it's important for men to bring up any concerns during doctor visits if she doesn't. "We say that everyone plays a role in the perinatal mood and anxiety disorder safety net and that husband, boyfriend, they're really on the frontline there."

Consider her family history. Even if your lady doesn't have a history of anxiety or depression, it's worth checking to see if there's any history of it in the family. Murdock says that some women never knew their mothers suffered from postpartum depression until they tell them about their own struggles. In other words: suggest that she ask her mom about it. If she struggled with it, your lady could, too.

Expecting to "have it all" can lead to some dark times. "The major myth of motherhood is that women need to be super mom and that they need to be perfect with everything," Murdock says. "What we find is that a lot of moms put a lot of pressure on themselves. They especially put a lot of pressure on themselves when they begin to go through a perinatal mood disorder. 'This isn't what I expected. How can this be happening to me?'"

Failure to breast-feed can lead to depression. Women who want to breast-feed but are unable to are more than twice as likely to get postpartum depression than women who never intended to breast-feed. Murdock says that sometimes when a woman is unable to breast-feed, it reinforces the idea that she is failing at her vision of what motherhood would look like. If your lady is unable to breast-feed, remind her that formula is a perfectly safe, acceptable, healthy option (see Week 25).

Yes, there are antidepressants and antianxiety medications pregnant and breast-feeding women can take. Murdock says many women simply stop taking their antidepressants when they find out that they're pregnant. She says there are some meds that are safe for fetuses (and babies if moms are breast-feeding), and to bring the issue up with their OB. This is serious stuff. Women with a history of depression are more likely to get prenatal and postpartum depression.

Week 15

Don't Let Her Microwave Bologna

Your baby has started sucking his thumb.

Your lady is scanning the Internet to find out what she can't eat or drink.

The situation: There's a laundry list of foods that are said to be off limits for pregnant women. They are even told to heat up deli meat in the microwave until steaming before consumption.

The reality: Don't let your lady put bologna in the microwave. Make her a toasted cheese and salmon melt, and ask her doctor to explain the real-world risks behind the foods she's told to avoid.

Near the top of a woman's worry list during pregnancy are the things that she's eating. One OB I spoke to told me she regularly gets calls in the middle of the night from patients concerned that they may have possibly eaten a piece of unpasteurized cheese.

Relax.

Yes, there's a good long list of foods (and drinks) that women are encouraged to stay away from while they're pregnant (and breast-feeding). But it's not as if these things turn into rat poison when your lady is pregnant. They're to be avoided, but they're not death pills.

Here's a look at some of the numbers behind common "do not eat" foods that might come in handy during a panic after a questionable lunch:

Soft Cheeses Made with Unpasteurized Milk and Deli Meats

Both of these are put on most "do not eat" lists because of an illness called listeriosis, caused by exposure to the listeria bacteria. Pregnant women are considered to be at a "higher risk" and the stat you might have heard is that they're ten times more likely to get listeriosis than the general population. That sounds worse than it is.

The Centers for Disease Control and Prevention estimate that 1,600 people will get listeriosis in the United States each year. Of these, 14 percent will be pregnant women. That means about 224 pregnant women will get listeriosis this year. There were almost four million babies born in the United States in 2013. Let's pretend that's the same number of pregnancies in the United States every year (though there were more, when you account for miscarriages). If 224 pregnant women get listeriosis, the risk of getting listeriosis is about one half of one hundredth of 1 percent, or roughly one in eighteen thousand. That number is actually high, considering there are more pregnancies than there are babies born. So, your lady has less than a one in eight thousand chance of getting listeriosis.

By comparison, a man's chance of getting breast cancer is one in one thousand, and more men will die of breast cancer this year (440) than pregnant women will get listeriosis. Every pregnant woman is worried about getting listeriosis, but I've never met a man worried about getting breast cancer.

Plus, of the reported listeriosis cases, many of them are associated with foods outside of the "do not eat" list, such as caramel apples and sprouts. According to the CDC, the largest listeriosis outbreak in US history occurred in 2011: 147 people got sick, 33 people died, there was 1 miscarriage, and it was caused by a bad batch of cantaloupe.

That President Brie she likes to eat with her Triscuits is probably just fine (yes, it's made with pasteurized milk). But deli turkey and the soft Mexican cheese—repeat offenders—might be best avoided. But if your lady realizes halfway through her sub that she accidentally got your turkey club, there is no reason to run to the ER.

Alcohol

In 2015, the American Academy of Pediatrics (AAP) declared that "no amount of alcohol intake should be considered safe" during pregnancy. That's different than saying the occasional glass of wine has been proven to be harmful—it has not. In fact, numerous studies through the years have observed that a couple drinks a week had no significant effect on babies.

When I spoke to one OB about this issue, she echoed the AAP's stance, and she mentioned that when she was pregnant, there was no societal pressure to drink. This is an interesting point. No pregnant woman should feel pressured to drink. If your lady chooses to abstain, don't be surprised if that annoying guy at the office happy hour trots out a study about the safety of alcohol. Fuck that guy. Even during pregnancy, women have the right to make their own choices about their bodies.

Fish

This is a really interesting one. The mercury found in fish can be bad for the unborn, but that doesn't mean women should avoid fish entirely. The omega-3 fatty acids found in fish are really good for women and their children (they help with brain development).

The economist Emily Oster put out a fascinating book called *Expecting Better* in 2013 that busts up some of the myths around all the danger warnings around pregnancy. Her section on off-limits food is a must read. Rather than casting a wide net across all fish—as the AAP is wont to do with all levels of alcohol—Oster analyzed the data to come up with a clever "Approval Matrix" for different fish, using the amount of mercury and omega-3 in each fish to chart their benefits and risks.

The results are pretty promising: tell her she can eat salmon, but should probably avoid tuna and orange roughy. But, hey, you can find canned salmon if she really wants a toasted cheese and fish melt.

But, again, even the off-limits fish aren't poison. If she eats a little, it's not like she's going to need to be rushed to the emergency room.

Ask her doctor specific questions about your lady's recommended diet. Don't just ask what she shouldn't eat. Ask what would happen if she accidentally ingested something from the naughty list. The answer—from a doctor she trusts—will go a long way on one of those nights that she's burrowed a deep hole in the Internet trying to find out if she's compromised her child.

week 16

Having a Baby Doesn't Change Everything

Your baby is moving enough that your lady might notice.

Your lady has started to tell people.

The situation: Most people tell you having a baby changes everything.

The reality: They're wrong. But if you're lucky, it will change many things.

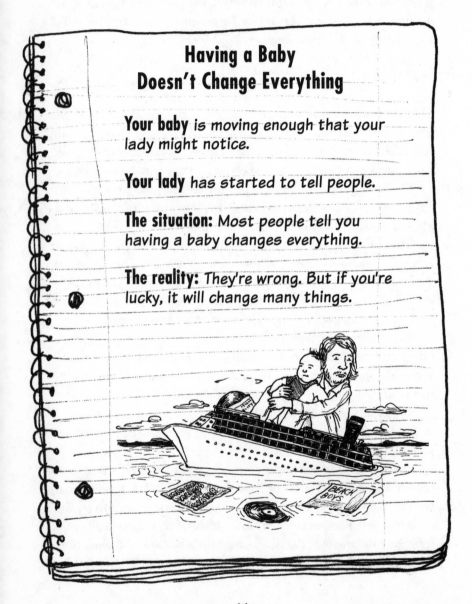

I know, by now you're hearing it every day, at least twice before lunch: "Having a baby changes everything." Don't listen to them. Babies can't change everything. They can't even change themselves.

Having a baby didn't even make me feel like an adult. It took a really bad concert to do that.

In 1997, when I was fifteen and Beck was at the height of his powers, I made my first trip to Bumbershoot, the Seattle music and arts festival when it was at the height of its powers, to see "Where It's At" performed on stage for my first time. I had no way of appreciating what a monumental occasion the evening would be for me, or the festival, but the show had ramifications (for both of us) that are still being sorted out today. And if you think I'm being hyperbolic, just ask the fire marshal or the folks who put on the festival.

Beck closed out Saturday night on the festival's biggest stage—an outdoor stadium where high-school football teams played on Friday nights. Unfortunately for me, Beck was playing just about the same time Cake was on stage across the festival grounds. Alexander, the older, "responsible" friend of the group wanted to see Cake the way I wanted to see Beck. So we struck the bargain that those of us who spent our youth with more ticket stubs than clean socks in our underwear drawer know well: we'd see the first half of one band (Cake), and sacrifice the first couple songs of the other (Beck).

The plan sounded strong, but this was my first experience at a summer music festival, and I had no idea how things worked. It was also, as I said, one of the most significant nights in Bumbershoot history. As we made our way to the stadium, we overheard an old guy (roughly the age I am today) mutter to our posse: "You're not gonna get in." This immediately sent me into a panic. And for good reason. When we got close to the gates, we saw a swarm—no, a legion—of fans trying to get in.

We were young and agile, and made our way toward the front of the group—losing my friend Robert in the process. We didn't have cell phones, of course. We just assumed we'd find him later.

When we got to the front, the picture came into focus. A handful of scraggly guards in yellow shirts were holding the crowd back from entering the stadium—literally with their arms. At one point Alexander and I heard a guy yell, "Let's just go!" The guards didn't stand a chance. We took the hill to the tune of "Devils Haircut." Just as Alexander and I were jumping for joy and high fiving each other, a dreadlocked cliché walked up to us and asked, "You guys need some fungus?" We were stumped. "You know, shrooms!" We passed.

That was the last year Bumbershoot worked the way it had for the preceding twenty years. In every subsequent year, admission to the main stage has been regulated, often by requiring a free wristband to get in. It's never been the same. To Bumbershoot and the fire marshal, I'm sure it's a good thing.

I really don't remember much about the concert. I remember "Devils Haircut." I remember "The New Pollution." And I remember leaving early to try to catch the 11:15 ferry home. But what I remember most vividly is the experience of getting inside, and the people I was with.

When it comes to going to a concert, or any other social and cultural gathering, the audience—your intimate circle and the greater tribe—matters infinitely more than the entertainment. That's why people go to the movies when they have Netflix, and why they go to concerts, even though, sonically speaking, they take place in rooms with the acoustic considerations of the sloppy side of a watermelon.

Regardless of the acoustic merits of that performance, Beck became my guy for life that night. Through the years I watched—always from a prime piece of real estate—as he reinvented himself album after album, tour after tour, and became the pop star whose evolution paralleled my teens and twenties.

I saw his band beat the shit out of a plastic Santa Claus in December of my senior year of high school; I saw him again a few months later, before graduation, this time rolling around in satin sheets on a giant brass bed while crooning "Debra." I listened to an advance copy of *Sea Change* at my desk at the *Argonaut*, horrified at what I heard. It was so different, so shocking, that before I was willing to accept its brilliance, it was almost incomprehensible.

But on May 28, 2012, at the Sasquatch! Music Festival—which has since overtaken Bumbershoot as the Northwest's most significant musical event—there was nothing new. He was an artist without momentum. He played the same songs I'd seen him play many times before. There was no innovation, no necessity for the performance. I had witnessed the most significant artist in my life transition from his most important offerings to the sameness that was to follow (that he won a Grammy three years later for *Morning Phase* says more about the Grammys than the artist).

When I saw Beck perform at Bumbershoot '97, I wasn't old enough to buy liquor or cigarettes; I wasn't eligible to vote; I couldn't join the army; I couldn't legally drive an automobile. By

the time Beck took the stage to close out Sasquatch! 2012, I'd gotten married, witnessed the birth of my first-born child, enrolled in a 401(k), said good-bye to my twenties, watched my house go underwater, seen my hairline retreat and my waistline expand. But none of these milestones felt as "you're not a kid anymore" as seeing the artist that was the linchpin of my musical development churn out a performance of pure nostalgia.

* * *

Three months after Beck deflated in front of my eyes at Sasquatch!, I was back at Bumbershoot. In the decade and a half since my first appearance, I'd missed only a couple years, even as the festival went in decline. Most of the years I was paid to attend, one of the many upsides to being a professional music journalist. They'd moved the main stage inside to an arena (a very bad idea), and in a case of very real déjà vu, I watched a hundred kids bum-rush security down a flight of stairs gunning for the floor during a set from the band M83. Part of me chuckled, part of me looked on in horror, and I wondered whether their shenanigans would change the festival forever.

Also on the festival grounds that weekend were Ben Blackwell—whose garage rock band the Dirtbombs were on the bill—and his wife Malissa, pregnant with their first child. Like me, concerts and shows act as mile markers in their lives.

The two met in Detroit on December 30, 1999, at a bar called the Old Miami. They both were under age. She was there to drink. He was there to see the band. He tried to get her to come back to see the show again the next night. She demurred because he was still in high school. He wore her down. Their first proper date was January 1, 2000.

Their paths had crossed before. She doesn't really remember, but he swears that they met when he was selling merch for his uncle's band—the White Stripes. From time to time he went on tour with Jack and Meg as they conquered the universe. She'd occasionally go on the road with friends' bands to sell merch or provide moral support. When they weren't working, they went to a lot of shows. That's just what they did.

They've been together, more or less, since we said good-bye to the nineties. A decade into the new millennium, they moved to Nashville so he could work at White's Third Man Records. A few months into the new job, he got a raise and a bonus: he bought a ring. Next up was a house, and, well, they figured it was time to have a kid.

Like every other couple with a kid on the way, they were inundated with the "having a baby changes everything" sermons, and they didn't have much patience for it. They were both adults. They wanted to start a family. They were ready for the next phase of their lives. Change was a promising proposition. But they weren't interested in saying good-bye to the life they'd built for themselves. They wanted to have a kid and a life.

Back in Detroit, none of their friends had kids. But in Nashville, they knew a couple named Todd and Jamie who unwittingly gave them the template for having a kid and a life at the same time. So, when Malissa gave birth to their daughter, Violet, they just decided to employ the Todd and Jamie Method.

Jamie Valentine was thirty-four when she became pregnant with her son, Townes. By then, she and Todd had been together for a decade, and they'd done a lot: they'd moved across the country, traveled, and otherwise checked off the to-do list of their twenties and early thirties. She was ready to make a baby. Todd wasn't quite so sure.

"I guess I'm kind of career-driven, or something similar to that," Todd told me. "And realizing there's going to be a lot of focus taken away from that, I think gave me some anxiety about it."

Neither of them wanted the baby to change everything. They wanted him to complement the life they were living. They still wanted to see their friends, go to concerts, and travel to see Jamie's family sprinkled around the United States and Canada. So, instead of letting Townes run the show, they just strapped him on and did, more or less, what they'd been doing before—as a trio.

When friends from Third Man got tacos after work, Todd and Jamie went along—and brought Townes. When their crew rented a cabin for a weekend, Townes was just one of the gang. Every year since he was born, Todd and Jamie have brought him to Gonerfest, an annual event put on by the Memphis garage rock label Goner Records. During the day they take him to shows— eleven months old on his first visit—and at night they leave him with friends or they all hang out together on a friend's porch.

It hasn't been completely seamless. When Townes was thirteen months old, they were asked to leave the patio at a Mexican restaurant called No Way Jose's Cantina because he was under age. To this day, Townes likes saying, "No way, Jose!"

Ben and Malissa soaked it all up.

"They showed us—whether they knew it or not—that your life doesn't stop because you have a kid. They just very, what seemed easily, integrated him into their life and into their social circle without this doom and gloom 'we had a baby, see you in eighteen years' mentality that seems to be what's laid out in books."

To be sure, both Ben and Todd have experienced the real changes that come with having a child. Even before Violet was born, Ben knew that his time was about to become far more precious. As a result, "unimportant shit just got shed."

He looked at his life and wondered what he could let go. He didn't have to look far. He was sick of going to shows.

"Fatherhood is the ultimate bullshit detector," he told me. "Once you're a parent, you can't suffer fools. You don't have time for bullshit. I like bands, but most of the time I leave a show unimpressed and kind of wishing I didn't go."

Ben says he doesn't see this as any kind of compromise, or proof that when you become a dad, your nights out instantly get wiped off the calendar. He says it's a matter of priorities and managing your resources—money, energy, time—giving up the things that don't matter and keeping the things that do.

"You adjust your worldview to accommodate things that are important to you," he said. "If it's really important to you or your job that you go out every night and know who the hit bands or DJs are or whatever, you're going to figure out a way to make that happen."

For Ben, his thing was buying records, which shouldn't come as a surprise, considering that he runs vinyl operations at Third Man and is the White Stripes's official archivist. Like all couples, he and Malissa tightened up their finances during the prebaby months. But they left money for LPs. "Because that's important to me, I've figured out whatever way to make sure that I still in some regard or another am able to do that."

Another change took Ben by surprise.

When thirty-two people died on board the Costa Concordia cruise ship in 2012, Ben remembers wondering how a person couldn't get out of there alive: the boat didn't even sink—it just listed—why not just jump off? "It seemed so easy to me. How could you not survive that?"

After Violet was born, the scene clicked into place. It made sense that a person could go down with the ship. It wasn't only him anymore. He couldn't just jump off and swim for it.

"Then it became: oh, shit, I can definitely see how someone would drown on a boat because you're dragging a three-year-old

along with you. My position on the most base primate level is
protecting this situation, this family. And that was something I
had not anticipated. And I don't think you can anticipate it until
you're actually there. It has to be a realization."

Dr. Scott Coltrane, a sociologist at the University of Oregon
who studies dads and families, notes that these kinds of instincts
don't only manifest in times of crisis. The daily parenting routine
of involved dads affects change on men as well.

"Men tend not to be as connected to other people," he says.
"Loving [your kids] and really wanting to do everything for them
makes one vulnerable. Serving them in a daily kind of way makes
you somewhat subservient to their needs and it makes you a better person, a more responsive person, and hopefully a better partner and spouse."

This is the big change that Todd felt when he became a dad.
Having Townes around has forced him to get out of his own
head, live in the here and now, and, yeah, basically think a little
less about himself.

"It has been a process for me to turn focus from myself to my
son and our family," Todd says. "I guess I'd tell other fathers to
open yourself up to the changes that are about to occur and you'll
be rewarded with a love that you never knew you were capable
of. For me, that has changed what life is truly about."

* * *

The first time I spoke to Ben, I was interviewing him for an article I
was writing about why CDs sound better than vinyl. When I found
out he was roughly the same age as me and had a daughter
roughly the same age as Thomas, I asked him what he thought
about the "having a baby changes everything" sermons. He chuckled and responded with a retort:

"Your whole life is going to change if you want it to."

The trick is deciding what to let change.

Week 17

Yes, Swaddling Is a Sport

Your baby is starting to put on some fat.

Your lady is starting to have some creative food cravings.

The situation: You're thinking about sleepless nights with a screaming baby.

The reality: Sleep well. Swaddle.

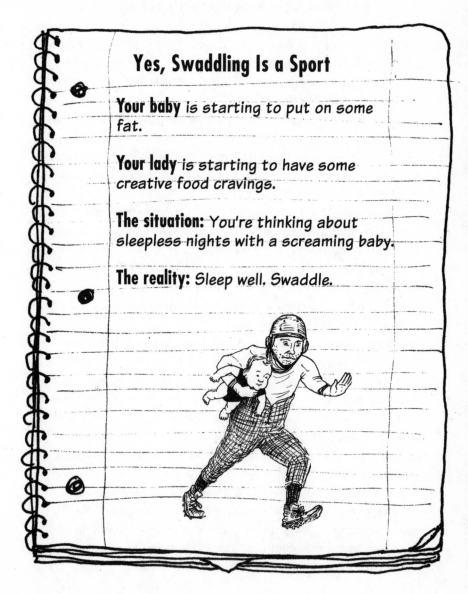

A side from "having a baby changes everything," the five words you're going to hear the most from friends, coworkers, and strangers on the bus are: "Remember, you absolutely have to . . ." followed by their secret parenting/baby-raising/newborn-surviving sauce. Everybody has one, and they're mildly miffed when you don't act on it. I'm pretty sure that my best friend, for example, is still disappointed in me for not doing the whole cosleeping thing.

Everybody's different. Every lifestyle is different. Everybody has different preferences (remember the Cake situation from last week). You're going to take and leave these nuggets as they come at you. Take the ones you want. Leave those you don't. It's totally up to you.

Except for this one. You can't leave this one on the table. If you want your child to sleep through the night—if you want to sleep through the night—you must try swaddling.

I know everyone's raising kids their own way. I know it's not fair to judge beyond what is reasonable for friends to judge each other, but when I find out a baby's not being swaddled, I want to grab her parents by the skull and slap them straight.

Both my kids were swaddled and both have slept like champs. Since she was eight weeks old, we've put Lucy—swaddled, naturally—in her crib around 7:30 every night, and fetched her—smiling, still swaddled—between 7 and 7:30 the next morning (these recent 4 a.m. mornings are the result of a cold, right?). I know every kid is different. I know she could just be a "good sleeper." And I'm not saying that it's anything we've done. I'm saying it's the swaddle.

It's not only for the child. Yes, it works like a charm. Your baby will sleep better than you ever thought possible. You'll be begging your lady to swaddle you up so you can experience the same. But, really, the best thing about swaddling is your entrance in the swaddling event in the fatherhood olympics.

Swaddling is the most enjoyable fatherhood activity this side of baby making. There's a unique satisfaction that comes from mastering the science of the swaddle, in wrapping a baby up so tight that they can't move their arms or legs, and turning a crying baby into a sleeping baby.

How tight is tight enough? You know how tight taco truck employees wrap those burritos? That's how tight you're going to wrap up your baby. Seriously.

And, no, there is no such thing as a good "loose" swaddle. That's an inadequate swaddle. That's a failed swaddle.

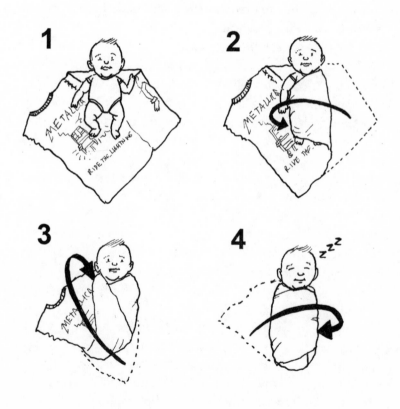

The idea behind swaddling is to provide the womb-like security of immobility, so don't let any arms escape because you think they "want" to keep their arms out. They want to sleep through the night. They want their arms out of the swaddle the way I want to eat the entire carton of cookies and cream.

I highly recommend doing some YouTubing to get your head around this process, but to start, see Aaron's rendering of a gold medal swaddle on the previous page.

P.S. If you can't get the hang of the swaddle—or want to make it just a little bit easier—buy a swaddler with Velcro. Every store has them. They're not quite as effective, but, if I'm being all kinds of honest here, they're pretty much what Lucy's grown up with. It's not cheating. It's practical.

Week 18

Shush Your Way to the Happiest Baby on the Block

Your baby is the size of a sweet potato.

Your lady has put on a dozen pounds and is starting to feel like a house.

The situation: You're still thinking about sleepless nights and screaming babies.

The reality: Tell her she's beautiful and shush your baby. Swaddling won't get you all the way home every time. Shushing your lady is not a good idea at any time.

T his is going to be an easy, but extremely important, week for both of us. Your homework is to watch a DVD.

I don't have a laundry list of baby paraphernalia to recommend. I'm not going to tell you that there's a compelling reason to bring a bassinet into your baby's life. But I will tell you this: if you want to be able to turn off your baby's tears, buy a copy of Dr. Harvey Karp's *The Happiest Baby on the Block* DVD. Study and learn.

I'm not going to give away too much, since his method can only be understood by watching the DVD. When I tell you what he does, you're not going to believe me, and that's OK. I didn't believe it till I saw it—till I tried it!—myself. It seems like voodoo. But it works.

Karp's method for getting a crying baby to come back to earth is five fold (as you get to know your baby, you'll learn which ones she responds to best, and you can start at different places):

Swaddling (natch). This is where you start. If a baby that's been fed, changed, and unharmed is all kinds of fussy, start by putting 'em in a swaddle.

Side/stomach position. If the swaddle doesn't work on its own, hold the baby on its side.

Shushing sounds. If the swaddle and side hold don't work, go in for the shush. Yes, it's just like what you think I said: "Shushhh-hhh" as loud as the baby is crying. It will turn them off like a switch does a light.

Swinging. If that doesn't work, you can start a little swinging. This is actually more like a light jiggle of the baby with one arm.

Sucking. Finally, if the baby's still worked up, stick in a pacifier, or offer up a finger for her to suck on.

I'm not giving anything away here. It doesn't make sense unless you watch him take a baby through the whole system. So, that's it for this week. Just watch the DVD, and don't feel like you can get out of it by scanning YouTube. Trust me, I've tried.

I know it seems a little early to be cramming this kind of thing, but don't procrastinate. Do it now before you're properly freaked out about shrieking children and sleepless nights. It will give you some confidence (plus, Karp demonstrates a killer swaddling technique!).

week 19

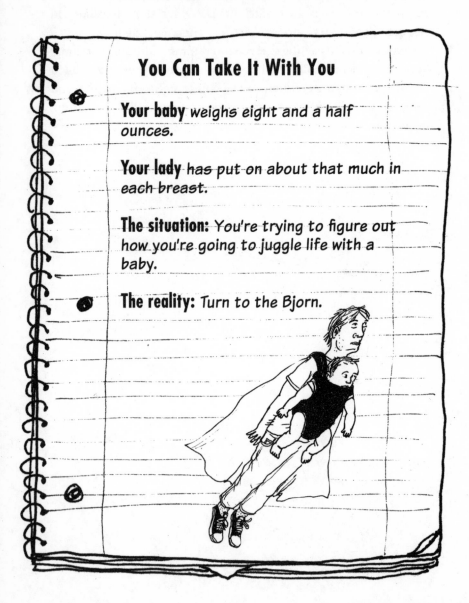

You Can Take It With You

Your baby weighs eight and a half ounces.

Your lady has put on about that much in each breast.

The situation: You're trying to figure out how you're going to juggle life with a baby.

The reality: Turn to the Bjorn.

*O*n the evening of Wednesday, August 23, 1995, my dad and I talked about going to see the Seattle Mariners play the New York Yankees the following afternoon. As games go, it didn't promise to be very compelling. The Mariners were, predictably, struggling. They had lost four out of their last five and were eleven games out of first place in the American League West. I seem to remember dad had a lot of work to do, and we went to a fair number of games, so we decided not to go.

But the following afternoon, dad called mom and told her to put me on the next ferry. If we hurried, he said, we could get there before the end of the first. We did. Just.

There was a small crowd—17,000—in the Kingdome that day, but enough to make a sizable roar when Jay Buhner hit a grand slam as we were making our way to our seats. This was promising. Then the Yankees made their move. By the bottom of the ninth, the Mariners were down nine to seven, the first two batters were easy outs and we started thinking about beating the crowd out of the dome.

Then Vince Coleman drew a walk. Then he stole second and, unsatisfied, proceeded to steal third. Joey Cora drove him in with a single to left. Down one, two out, and a man on first, Ken Griffey Jr. took the plate.

* * *

My dad taught me how to go to concerts by taking me to baseball games. When I became a teenager and going to concerts became my thing, dad gamely exercised that part of himself and we went to many concerts together—the 1999 Bob Dylan/Paul Simon co-headlining tour being one of our first. But in the eighties and early nineties, we went to games together, usually with my mom and brothers. But he also made a point of taking his sons one at a time.

I was about eight the first time my mom put me on the ferry by myself to meet dad after work and go see a game. I had strict instructions to walk directly off the boat and find dad on the other side before we walked to the Kingdome. I can still remember searching for his face in the awaiting throng and spotting it as the boat pulled into the dock.

I never considered my dad strict or unreasonable. But he had standards. When we were out and about, we were expected to keep it clean, to mind our business, to pick up after ourselves, and, for lack of a better description for the reasonable expectations of an eight- or nine-year-old, to be professional.

Duff has often reminded me that I'm parenting right now, when my kids are in single digits and it seems like they aren't listening. Right now is when I'm teaching them how to make good decisions. When Thomas is a teenager, he says, my role will be largely over. Looking back at my own upbringing, I can see his point.

Dad never told me: "Hey, pay attention, this is how you get to the stadium from the ferry." I just walked with him and remembered. He never told me: "I'm teaching you how to do this so you can do it yourself one day." I just absorbed it. He told me not to act out. To sit up straight. To not dress like a slob. He didn't explicitly say: "This is so you don't look like an easy target." But that's the lesson. He taught me how to conduct myself in public.

I was eleven the first time I went into Seattle—the big city— without an adult. It wasn't supposed to be that way. I was supposed to go to the game with my summer friend, Jonathan, and his dad, a former member of the US House of Representatives who had what I assumed to be free time on his hands, since he had recently lost his bid for the Senate. But when Mrs. Former Congressman approached her husband, he replied: "I'm not going to spend all day at the ballpark!" He told her to send the kids by themselves. My mother, kind of surprised, didn't balk at the congressman's declaration (even though he was a Democrat, and she was constitutionally obligated to object to every one of his opinions).

Riding the ferry and making our way through Seattle's heroin-sprinkled streets—past the famous OK Hotel, where Nirvana had debuted "Smells Like Teen Spirit" a few years earlier—I never once thought: Dad taught me how to do this. We just did it, made it to the Dome, and enjoyed the game without incident. Thereafter, I was allowed to go to games in Seattle without an adult, allowing former congressmen everywhere to spend a little less time with their sons during the week.

* * *

I think that because I grew up with kids who weren't allowed to (and didn't have the savvy to) go into the city—or cut their own meat—until after they got their driver's licenses, I've fixated on Dad's unwitting lessons on public transportation and conduct. It's important to me that Thomas and Lucy grow up to be savvy, to be the kids who can get around and aren't afraid to hop the bus or ferry.

Every dad will have his own thing. I can't change the oil in my car or fillet a fish, but I can see how those would be important skills for some dads to pass down to their daughters and sons.

From the day he was born, Thomas and I have been bumming around Seattle. Infants, despite what you've heard, are extremely portable. They lead a delightfully slothful existence. They eat, sleep, and dirty diapers. But as long as they're getting some sleep, eating enough, and you're changing those diapers, you can pretty much take them anywhere. And, yes, they sleep in strollers, can be changed in the McDonald's restroom, and can be fed on the park bench. In other words: they're far more agreeable than most of your friends—they won't request Cake over Beck (as long as you've raised them right, at least).

Our adventures started at the record store. At the time of his birth, we lived, conveniently, a mile down the road from a shop with a killer bargain bin. So, it was a regular Saturday-afternoon affair for me to toss him into the Bjorn while Betsy was at work and wander down the street to take a chance on a two-dollar Charlie Rich LP. Eventually, we got more adventurous, and I tried getting Thomas into Hollywood.

One Friday night, as I was walking home late to our apartment, nestled between hospitals and the aftermarket pill pushers who operate out of their wheelchairs, I came upon an apartment building filled with floodlights. I assumed a drug bust, but in fact it was a little slice of tinsel town on our corner of Pill Hill. I lingered for a few moments until a dude in a headset took a break, and I asked him what was going on. *Fat Kid Rules the World*, he told me. I guess it's a popular kids' book that was being turned into a movie by Matthew Lillard, the guy from *Scream* who played the main killer's sidekick (you know, the spaz). They'd be shooting for two weeks.

A couple days later, the crew was still getting down to business—I even spotted Lillard in the alley making grand gestures with both arms. The help was instructing passersby when to walk past the downstairs window on command, so, I inquired: "Need any extras?"

I was in luck. They didn't need any more at the time, but they needed some around noon the next day. I was visibly excited to the point that a grip or whoever told me: "I love how excited you are about this."

Next question: "Can I wear my six-month-old in a Bjorn when I walk by the window tomorrow?"

"Sure," he said. "If you want to bring a baby, that's fine with me."

Perfect.

The next day, Thomas and I got ready. We each bathed and wore clean shirts. I wore my red Ray-Ban Wayfarer sunglasses that I got at Fred Meyer with the company insurance; Thomas wore blue shades with a pacifier accent. As we made our way down to the set, a grip (or whoever)—a different one this time around—saw us coming. Grinning, he asked us what we were up to.

"We're here to be extras," I told him, not even trying to contain my excitement. "We were told to be here at noon!"

"Oh . . . sorry . . . "

They were done with extras for the day. They were pretty much done shooting. They loved our glasses, though.

I was disappointed, but I felt worse for Thomas. My only consolation is that I was able to use the opportunity as a teaching moment: Hollywood is a fickle bitch.

* * *

Now that we live across the water from Seattle, it's Thomas's turn to learn the ways of the ferry lifestyle/mentality that my father passed down to me. We started basic, going to a Mariners's game. He fell asleep in left field and I carried him—asleep—all the way back to the ferry. But that was just the warm-up. After he turned three, I figured he was ready for his first Bumbershoot.

To get to Bumbershoot from our house, we have to take the bus, then the ferry, then walk through downtown Seattle and catch a monorail that drops us off at the festival grounds. I wasn't dreading the logistics, but it felt like a lot of hoops to jump through for a kid to see some live music.

Thomas ate it up. He has always loved taking the ferry, getting snacks at the concession stand, watching the boat take off. He loved walking through the city and taking in the sights, and he loved riding the monorail for the first time.

Once we made it to campus, Thomas ate an ice-cream cone while we watched an uninspiring hip-hop performance on the lawn. When the ice cream was gone, we went inside to check out one of the bands on my cheat sheet. We saw exactly one song before Thomas gave me the signals that he was ready to go home. No problem. We turned around, hopped on the monorail, walked back through town to the ferry terminal, boarded the boat, sailed for an hour, and caught our bus home. Thomas loved it. He thinks the Seattle Center grounds is Bumbershoot. Catching a ferry, walking through the city, and riding the monorail is a freaking carnival for a three-year-old.

Yes, it was a short stay at the festival. No, I didn't care. We could have seen more. There could have been a stroller involved. Betsy could have come along, and Thomas could have taken a nap on a blanket to recharge his battery. In the end, the concert was about as material for me as it was for Thomas.

Concerts have always been more about company than music. And by that measure, it was one of the best Bumbershoots I'd ever been to.

* * *

I think about my dad every time Thomas and I are on a public adventure. Surely going to Mariners's games with his kids was a different experience for him than when he went with clients or friends from work. To this day, I've never once seen my dad drink a beer at a Mariners's game. But I promise you my dad's had a couple at the ballpark. I know he never felt like it was a compromise, bringing my brothers and me. He never grumbled or pined for the good old days when he went to games with his buddies rather than with kids who pestered him for souvenirs in the bottom of the second. It was a different experience, and one that he loved.

I still think about those games today, especially that one in 1995.

Two out, one run down and Joey Cora on first, Griffey didn't take the first pitch—he launched it over the right-field wall.

The Mariners played their first game on April 6, 1977. But until 1995, they'd never made the postseason. That win, that home run, has been credited with sparking the Mariners's remarkable 1995 comeback that saw them win their division for the first time. It was a historic game that dad just couldn't stand not taking me to.

Two decades later, Griffey returned to the Mariners to get a season or two in at the twilight of his career. Lots had changed. You could say everything had changed, and it had nothing to do with having a baby. The Kingdome was imploded to make way for a football stadium, and the Mariners had a home with a retractable roof next door. This time, I was the one hustling up the tickets.

It was the first game of the season we'd seen and I was feeling more than a little nostalgic to go back and see Griffey with my dad, as we'd done countless times when I was a kid. We were both disappointed to learn that Griffey wasn't in the lineup.

The game went about as well as could be expected, which is to say the M's did just about nothing, going scoreless through seven innings. Then in the eighth, the Mariners started to show some life. Our seats looked directly into the Mariners's dugout. I could see the batter on deck taking his practice swings. Down by two, with one man on, I could see the pinch hitter come from behind and tap the batter on the shoulder. The whole crowd knew who it was. And when Griffey approached home plate, everyone rose to their feet.

Ken Griffey Jr. is the best baseball player in Mariners's history— the best athlete in the history of Seattle sports. He is the reason the Mariners got a new ballpark and weren't sold out of state. In his injury-prone later years, he didn't have the same juice. But some things were the same as they ever were. Like that August afternoon in 1995, he still only needed one pitch. Only this time he didn't take it to right, he put it over the center-field wall.

Dad was emotional. I was emotional. Griffey tipped his hat. For a minute, it was 1995. I was thirteen. And neither of us wanted to be anywhere other than in the stands, together, watching Ken Griffey Jr. bring a crowd to a boil.

My dad worked hard (he still does!). He commuted for four hours a day, left the house at 4:30 a.m. and didn't see us until it was about time for dinner. And he was there for us.

His feeling—You know what, dammit, I've got a lot of work to do today, but I can't stand not going to the game with my son—was palpable. It made me feel like the only other person in the world. I can still feel it. It's what I remember most about the game. And I'm proud to say that I inherited the sentiment, and have felt it for Thomas.

After the Seahawks won the Super Bowl in 2013, the city threw an enormous homecoming parade. I had considered taking the day off work and taking Thomas, but didn't pull the trigger. On the bus, on the way to the ferry on the morning of the parade, I couldn't stand it. I texted my boss and got the day off. I called Betsy and told her I was coming home to pick up Thomas so we could throw Skittles at Marshawn Lynch. Then the bus got to the ferry terminal. I've never seen anything like it. In my life, I've never missed a ferry because it was at capacity—had never heard of it happening. Not only were we not getting on that boat, there were so many people trying to get to the parade we'd have to wait another two hours before we'd be able to catch a ride to town. We didn't make it.

Yes, my heart was broken. And this was another big league disappointment for Thomas. I'm just praying he was too young to remember that his old man doesn't know how to get into the movie business or homecoming parades, and that it's enough that he can find his way to the monorail.

Listen to Laura Veirs

Your baby can hear your voice, but has not picked a side in the Stones/Beatles debate.

Your lady likes No Doubt.

The situation: You haven't liked No Doubt since 1997. Hearing it today makes you retch.

The reality: Kids' music is much worse. You need to be prepared.

If you've spent any amount of time shopping for baby-related items, you're well aware that there is no commercial prospect left unexploited. Passing over any of them can give you your first feelings that you're not doing enough for your child.

Music for infants is no exception. A cottage industry has grown around providing infant-appropriate, sleep-inducing versions of popular music. They are, almost without exception, excruciating. In another corner of humanity these discs are used as torture devices.

Wade carefully. Introducing music to your child is a lifelong decision. A smarter man than myself recently put it this way: don't expose your children to music unless you are willing to hear it a dozen times in a row. This, of course, I can attest to. I've already told you about Thomas's Nirvana phase (no complaints here). Yesterday I spent the better part of a half hour listening to Billy Joel's "Uptown Girl" on repeat (again, it's all good).

Not only is baby music bad, but it's redundant. Your record collection (or Spotify account) has everything your child needs. Steer clear of music targeted for infants, and just find some mellow jams that you can tolerate. Don't waste your money on *Rockabye Baby! Lullaby Renditions of Radiohead*. Just turn on Radiohead. You'll both be catching up on your sleep in no time. A favorite of mine is *Getz/Gilberto*. I have sent my babies to sleep many times to the tune of "The Girl From Ipanema." They lose themselves in the lush tones of Stan Getz's saxophone. Their eyes roll back, lids close and you don't have to listen to baby Muzak to get there.

Before I knew about the baby-music misnomer, I started absorbing kid records from time to time. One of the perks of being a music editor was CDs and LPs just showed up at my desk. One, from the indie, critical darling Laura Veirs caught my eye. *Tumble Bee*, an album of old folks songs for kids, wasn't campy like the rest of the kiddie crap, so I brought it home.

I, more or less, forgot about it, but Betsy didn't. And I have many fond memories of her rocking Thomas to sleep to the words "come on, horsey, hey, hey . . . " The album isn't a piece of the infant music marketing machine. It's an album for kids that—like albums for adults—our family found soothing.

I called Ms. Veirs to say thank you, to ask her what she thought of music for kids and babies, and why she ended up making the album in the first place.

"I can't remember exactly why we made the record," she said. "My memory has gone out the window since I had kids, that's one thing. My brain gets used for so many different things, there are certain things I just can't retain anymore."

Fair enough.

"I think the main reason we did it was I just didn't want to write at that time. I felt so taxed psychologically, emotionally, and physically after having my son that I was like: 'I'm just going to do a record for kids, because there isn't that much great new music for kids out there, and I don't want to write right now.'"

Since she didn't want to write, the album is made up almost entirely of covers. Some of the songs are ones her parents sang to her when she was a child. Others are ones that her parents heard when they were growing up. Veirs plucked several of the songs for the album off Peggy Seeger's *Animal Folk Songs for Children*, an album with charming numbers about bees and butterflies pecking the eyes out of dead animals. She liked the dark material, and she thinks it's important for kids to know that we're part of the cycle of life.

"It was neat to put myself in that flow, that river of old folk music. And not be too pansy about it. And be like: Yeah, we're going to sing about these real things because we always have. And we shouldn't just sugarcoat everything for kids."

For the record, she hasn't heard *Lullaby Renditions of Radiohead*, but she doesn't think it's a good idea. "Kids just love music, so we can put on anything and they love it. They don't need kids' music."

While I had Veirs—now a mother of two—on the phone, I asked her for some tips for new dads and her thoughts on things she'd do differently. Here's what she said:

Don't worry about being perfect. "Somehow I drank the Kool-Aid. I was, like, no formula, that's just not allowed. It made it really difficult because I was touring with the baby and, like, breast-feeding in the car. I was like: 'I can't do that, it's terrible.' It's not terrible. So, the second time around I gave my baby some formula so I didn't have to stress out on tour with my baby. The babysitter took him to the hotel, gave him a bottle of formula, he went to bed, no big deal. He's fine. There's as many different ways to do things as there are people on earth. Teenagers used to raise us, because that's when you had kids. You had kids when you were like nineteen or thirteen. They figured it out. Just take a chill pill. We're all gonna be OK."

What's best for the baby is whatever's best for the family. "If the mom and dad are happy, then the kids are gonna be happy. And if the mom and dad want to work, then go to work. If you want to be home, be home. If you have the flexibility to make some kind of compromise between those two things, you're really lucky."

Be sympathetic; she's more tired than she looks. "Especially in the first trimester, you just look normal. You don't even look pregnant, but it is so exhausting. And it's hard for other people, especially men, to relate to that. Extend your empathy. Dig a little deeper. Do that extra load of laundry and the extra chores that might be piling up because she's taking a nap. Stepping up a little bit in that regard is a big help to the woman so she can just feel a little more relaxed and not have to keep up with every little thing."

Hearing that last bit stung a little. I can vividly remember getting frustrated with Betsy when she overextended herself cleaning the shower in her last week of pregnancy. At the time, I thought she was being unreasonable, pushing herself too far. And she was. But that was my fault. I know she and I have different definitions of cleanliness. I know she likes things to be picked up. I know she's going to try and do it herself even if she shouldn't. But I wasn't very proactive. I didn't acknowledge that it was my responsibility to not let her put herself in that position. I didn't, as Veirs suggested, step it up and allow her to feel more relaxed, to feel good about taking a nap and taking care of herself.

Neither of these situations is going away after your baby is born. As Veirs says, picking up the slack during pregnancy is just the beginning of "infinite tasks and unending chores. It never ends."

Neither does the kid/baby music-marketing machine. On both fronts, you've got to be proactive. And do your homework.

If, for example, you've managed to keep the *Frozen* soundtrack out of your childless universe, stream it a couple times before you decide to expose your children to it. Because once you do, they'll never let it go. You're not being selfish. You're being strategic. If it doesn't make you happy, it's not making anybody happy. Veirs is right: "What's best for the kids is whatever's best for the family."

"Let It Go" might not be good for your family.

Week 21

Listen to Caspar Babypants

Your baby has taste buds.

Your lady can no longer hide the fact that she's pregnant.

The situation: You don't know the first thing about parenting.

The reality: That's OK. Start by scheduling some regular dad time into your postbirth plans.

*O*ne of the last pieces of advice Laura Veirs told me she'd pass along to new parents is to ask for help. Whatever it is. If you can afford a babysitter, hire one when you need it. If you need a meal, don't be shy about sending up a signal to your friends and loved ones.

I think that advice extends to asking for advice. Ask other men how they did it. Ask people you trust and people you don't. You're not going to take everyone's advice, but bits and pieces are going to resonate with you. Ultimately, I don't think figuring out your parenting or work-life scheme is about perfecting a million different things: I think it's about finding the few things that make fatherhood and life with kids work for your family.

I'm not writing a book about how to parent. And, as Veirs said, there are as many ways of being a parent as there are parents in this world. So if you want to find a "style" of raising children, I'd direct you back toward the parenting section of your local bookstore (please don't exchange this book).

When I found out Betsy was pregnant, I immediately started working questions about parenting and fatherhood into conversations I had at work. And since I was working as a music editor, that meant I asked a fair number of rock and rollers how they dadded.

A local club booker told me the best thing I could do for my pregnant wife was "just be there." Asked what he would do if his son grew up to be a Yankees fan, The Strokes's Julian Casablancas told me that "he'll have his share of bad choices that he'll have to make on his own that I can't help him with."

Since Thomas was due on Halloween, and we'd been calling our unborn child Casper, I thought it appropriate to write an article based around fatherhood tips solicited from Presidents of the United States of America's Chris Ballew, who records kids' music under the Caspar Babypants moniker (which, it must be said, bucks the kids' music stereotype, and I highly recommend). I still think back to that conversation often. Here's what he told me:

So, what parenting tips do you have?

Ballew: I think the blanket, big-picture advice I would have for parents is learn to be empathetic, and acknowledge what your kids say. You don't always have to say yes, but acknowledge what they say, and hear them, and let them know you heard them—and I think you can eliminate a lot of stressful interactions through simple empathy.

What about advice for brand-new fathers, from, say, day 1 to day 101?

What I did is I got up every morning with my baby. I was the morning-duty guy. And that was incredibly awesome time, and really mellow and quiet and watching the sun come up with the baby in your arms and falling asleep again on the couch and feeding it and kind of bonding with the baby during the morning hours. I did that with both my kids their entire childhood. I just love those memories.

Before you started making music for kids as Caspar Baby-pants, when you were raising your kids, was there any music in particular that they responded really well to?

Yeah, mine. I used to lay them out on a blanket and just play guitar and improvise songs for them. And they responded to them great. Of course, I recorded them all as I did them, so I have all these fragments—the blanket sessions, as I call them—and some of those are turning into great Caspar songs. They [also] responded to classical music and the Beatles and a *Sesame Street* collection of hits lying around that they loved. They liked it all.

Disposable or reusable diapers?

There's no conclusive evidence as to which one is more taxing on the environment. So for pure convenience, and lack of touching poo, which you do a lot as a parent, I'd go disposable.

How do you feel about Bjorns?

Oh, I love them. I love seeing little babies coming toward me, all kicking and looking around. They're just hilarious.

Is there an indispensable baby/parenting accessory?

Oh, the little bouncy swingy thing that claps into the doorway. It's kind of a sling with leg holes that you put the baby in and they can kind of bounce around while you're in the kitchen making dinner. That thing is killer.

week 22

It's OK. Nobody Else Knows How They're Going to Make It Work, Either

Your baby has fully-formed eyelids and eyebrows.

Your lady is beginning to talk about painting the baby's room.

The situation: You're wondering how you're going to afford daycare and/or the lack of a second income.

The reality: You have options. Consider all of them. Especially the ones you detest.

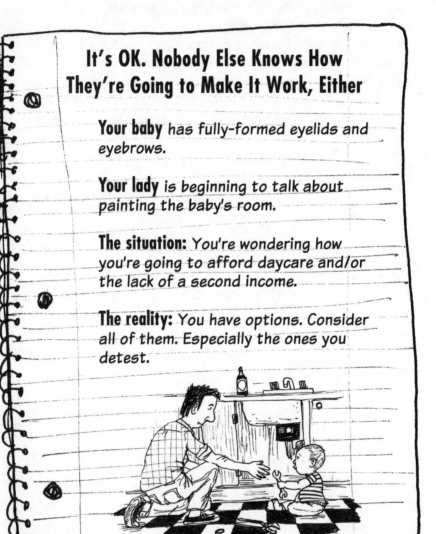

I have a complex about two things: leaving food on my plate and sending my kids to daycare. I've never left a scrap on my plate, but a few months after Thomas's first birthday, I left him with strangers. I sobbed. Couldn't stop.

I don't know why I've got a problem with daycare. I have no reason to have a problem with daycare. In my life, I actually don't think I've ever heard a horror story about daycare, or talked to someone who thought going to daycare stained his soul. The only reason why I might be repulsed by the idea of daycare is because I never spent a day there. I hung out with my mom and brothers until it was time to go to school. And even then I spent as much time away from school as possible. I had half-day kindergarten and can vividly remember being late to a field trip because my mom and I were out on a spectacular adventure at the park behind the grocery store—an adventure that would be matched, for a six-year-old, only by the sensation of walking, alone, to my classroom to find it dark and empty (this was 1988, when six-year-olds were still allowed to walk, unaccompanied, through halls in search of dark, empty rooms).

When I dropped Thomas off at daycare that first day, and settled him down in front of some blocks, I hugged him and kissed him and apologized for leaving him—and I meant every word of it. I was convinced I was abandoning him. I was convinced I was robbing him of precious toddler time with his mom and dad.

Whether you're a millionaire or living hand to mouth, all parents struggle to make it work. Even if you can afford full-time childcare, there's no way you can be in two places at once. You're either with your child or you're not. All the money in the world can't bridge that gap. Nothing can prepare you for what it feels like to have to choose between taking your child to daycare, hiring a nanny, or putting a career on hold while you or your lady stay home. It's a juggle and a struggle for everyone, a Rubik's Cube that changes color every time you give it a turn.

When Betsy went to work part-time, I worked a couple half days from home each week, so that we could avoid daycare, and I could spend time with Thomas while Betsy brought in some cash and reacquainted herself with the adult side of the human race. Ballew was right: these times are invaluable. There's no substitute for having time alone with your child. When mom's in the room, they know mom's in the room. So, our days went something like this:

I took Ballew's advice and took the morning shift. I woke up with Thomas around six, and we played and messed around in the living room for the better part of two hours while Betsy caught up on her sleep. If I left our bedroom door closed, Thomas would forget that Betsy was in there, and I had him all to myself.

On days that Betsy worked an afternoon shift at a retailer in town, I left the house around eight and came home after lunch. Thomas and I infant wrestled and he sucked on plastic rings when he was awake. When he was asleep—and God bless him, he rocked a solid three-hour midday nap for a long time—I flipped open my laptop and got to work. When Betsy got home and we had Thomas in bed, I'd flip the computer back on and wrap up my day. Then we'd fall asleep and start the dance all over again.

When we moved back to our house in Bremerton, everything shifted. It's always shifting.

I was able to swing a shift a week from home, and Betsy found a half-time job at the local community college. To make it work, we knew we'd have to bite the bullet and send Thomas to daycare for the twenty hours a week that Betsy worked. It hurt.

After the blubbery first day, things got progressively easier. Day two was tough, but not quite as bad.

The next week worked, but I still felt inadequate, embarrassed, and ashamed that, unlike my dad, I didn't make enough money to afford for him to stay home all day with his mom. But it didn't take long for me to get to the point I'm at now: grateful for daycare and convinced that it was the best thing for Thomas and our family.

Like I said, I had zero experience with daycare, and had no idea what to expect, other than that he'd be bringing home a petri dish of germs and expletives. He brought home a lot more. It was amazing, shocking even, how much he developed socially by being around other kids for half the day. It was incredible how much he advanced when we weren't around. They had him clearing his own plate in a week. It's hard for new parents to know when their kids are ready to do things for themselves. But at daycare, when there's a dozen kids in the room, it's a necessity.

I'm sure a lot of this is me justifying our decision—which I'm happy to do. But the improvements we saw were not only anecdotal. It turns out daycare offers real benefits for kids. A 2006 study put out by the National Institutes of Health's National Institute of Child Health and Human Development noted that "children in higher quality nonmaternal childcare had somewhat better language and cognitive development during the first four and a half years of life." On the other hand, the study also noted that kids who go to childcare centers "also showed somewhat more behavior problems in childcare and in kindergarten classrooms than children who experienced other nonmaternal childcare arrangements."

Dr. Jim Griffin, one of the top experts on all things kids at the National Institutes of Health, says benefits on both sides are modest. Griffin says the child's family—"everything from genetics through the environment, through social class, through culture, through all of the other things that come bundled up with that" —has a much greater impact.

"Whether you are in out-of-home care from infancy or you're home with your mother from infancy," Griffin says, "the family still has much more impact than the choice of childcare."

There's no perfect solution, only the right solution for you and your family. And every family—not that I'm telling you anything you don't know—does things differently. To demonstrate the wildly different possibilities, here's a look at how three other families I've encountered in the last year are making it work.

Paul Franklin,
Oscar-Winning Visual Effects Supervisor

I first spoke with Paul Franklin in early 2015, just a few days before he brought home an Oscar for his visual effects work on the Matthew McConaughey vehicle *Interstellar*. During our brief chat about the gear that he can't live without, I learned that some of his most indispensable pieces of technology were those that kept him in touch with his wife and three kids back in London. As he explained later, being an involved father while working in the film business takes its own kind of creativity.

Paul and his wife, Jane Burton, both have demanding, full-time jobs. When Jane was expecting their first child she was working as a curator at the Tate Modern museum in London and Paul was wandering around Prague working on 2003's *The League of Extraordinary Gentlemen*, a film that's somewhat famous in Hollywood for being something of a handful. The fact that its visual effects supervisor was expecting his first child and that his house was being remodeled at the same time wasn't the problem. Apparently there were issues with the script and Sean Connery didn't get along with the director, among other peccadilloes.

Paul and Jane both enjoy their jobs (Jane now works for a large auction house) and had no plans to put either on hold once they started a family. To help juggle a family and two demanding jobs Jane and Paul employ a part-time nanny, a situation that he says has worked out well. He says it's important not only to find the right nanny, of course, but to be vigilant, to not think that because you have picked someone to take care of your kids, things then go on cruise control. But when you find the right person, he says, it can be like having another member of the family.

"I think some people worry that if they bring another person into the house that they may be somehow dividing the love of their children amongst a wider pool of people and somehow they're not going to get loved as much as they would have been otherwise. But, I don't think that's the case at all. Children have a huge amount of love in their hearts and there's plenty to go around."

The nanny can help with the logistics of raising three young kids, but Paul never thought his role was being filled in his absence. There was still parenting to do. Though Jane is understanding of Paul being away from home for long periods of time for work, the kids are a different matter. It isn't that they are not understanding. It's that they forget.

"Sometimes you're lucky and you're only spending a couple of weeks away from home, and I don't think that is too hard to deal with at all. But when it stretches beyond a month and if it's something that's on a regular basis, I began to realize that unless I made real efforts to get on the phone with the kids, that they kind of forgot about you. A child's perception of the way that time passes is very different from an adult."

Early on in his kids' lives, he did what he could to keep in touch. There were phone calls home at first, whenever possible. And later, he moved on to Skype. But Internet speeds around the world didn't make Skype manageable until after his third child was born and he was working on the 2012 film *The Dark Knight Rises* when things finally caught up with where they should be.

While the film was shooting in California, he found time to get away from the set in the mornings (evening back home in London), to chat with his kids on Skype. He says he'd often read two of his kids a bedtime story while Jane put one of the others to bed. On the weekends, he'd stay in at his hotel and catch up with his kids while his colleagues were enjoying the West Coast.

"I'd regularly get back to the set on a Monday and people would ask, 'So, what were you up to this weekend?' They'd gone snowboarding at Big Bear or riding bikes through Topanga Canyon and I'd say, 'Well, you know, I stayed in and read a story to my kids on the Internet.' But it was totally worth it, because when I got back home after the film had wrapped, I realized that while it wasn't exactly the same as if I'd been at home all the time, I'd managed to maintain a relationship with my kids. They still remembered who I was. And we were talking about the same things—things I was talking about were things that were current in their world."

Every film has presented its own challenges and opportunities. While shooting *Interstellar* on a glacier in Iceland—which they used as one of the planets in the film—service was so bad they may as well have been on Mars, though he was able to get a few Skype calls in from his iPhone and some proper chats back at the hotel. While on break in Canada during the shooting on the film, Paul found that he got fantastic service at the local dinosaur museum. So, instead of reading his kids a bedtime story that day, he gave them an impromptu tour of the museum via Skype on his phone.

"What you realize is that you have to make an effort. It's not something that just happens automatically or happens spontaneously. It's not as if you just walk in through the front door of the house and into the living room or the kitchen and your kids wander in. You have to make time. You have to essentially make an appointment in your day to have this interaction with your family. And if you don't do it, it isn't going to happen on its own."

Aaron (the illustrator), Jessixa (the illustrator) and Baxter (the charmer)

In the weeks and months leading up to the birth of his son, Baxter, Aaron Bagley had a vision in his head of what fatherhood would look like, how he and his wife would juggle two work lives and one new life. He remembers being anxious, excited, and champing at the bit, thinking, "I just want the baby on me, and to be vacuuming."

Aaron, if you haven't already made the connection, is the illustrator behind the drawings you see in this book. When he's not illustrating books, he's cartooning for the local alt-weeklies. When he doesn't have a pencil in his hand, his tools of choice include plungers, wrenches, and a calculator.

Aaron and I met when I was editing at *Seattle Weekly* and I commissioned both he and his wife, Jessixa, to do some work in the music section. Like all resourceful freelance artists, Aaron's figured out a way to make art and make a living. A few years ago, just as he was considering dusting off his resume to look for a standard nine-to-five, the manager of his apartment building told him he was moving on, and would he be interested in managing the building? Of course. He was already picking up shifts at a local used bookstore, and between the three jobs—freelancing, book buying, and apartment managing—he'd cobbled together a gig. Then he got Jessixa pregnant.

"I think it was just sort of unspoken that I was gonna take care of him because I had this schedule, this work life that I had created for myself that was super ideal for just how I am as a person," he says. "You throw a kid in there and he just becomes a part of your routine."

Their routine is that there isn't a routine. There are always changes at the apartments. Tenants come and go, light fixtures break, drains get clogged. As soon as Jessixa went back to work, his paternity vision became a reality.

In the morning, the two hang out and listen to records. When Baxter's asleep or eating lunch, Aaron gets a little sketching done. When it's time to manage the building, he brings along his associate.

He straps Baxter into the Ergo (baby carrier) when he vacuums, brings him on calls when sinks need to be fixed, and lets him crawl around the floors of apartments as he shows them to prospective tenants.

"And he's the best buffer for kind of crabby apartment tenants," Aaron says. "They see him and they see me and that I'm coming to do some dumb thing for them, and they are so nice to me."

It's been the same story at the bookstore. Aaron's on the schedule every Wednesday and picks up shifts occasionally throughout the week. When he goes in, he straps Baxter on and does his duty, buying and selling at Seattle's Mercer Street Books. Baxter does his part, too, charming the eclectic crowd that populates the neighborhood.

"I've had some people say: you guys have a bookstore baby, that's way better than a bookstore cat," says Debbie Sarow, the store's owner. "It adds a vibrancy to the bookstore that's nice for people to experience."

Baxter usually stays with Aaron for an hour or two, and then Jessixa gets off work early and picks him up, and Aaron finishes up his shift. After dinner, they put Baxter down, clean up, pour drinks, and get out their pencils. When they can't stay awake any longer, they shut off the lights and say goodnight to the city, of which they have a panoramic view from their two-bedroom apartment. Yes, two-bedroom apartment.

When they told people they were pregnant, they all asked: "You're gonna move, right?" Aaron says that they could move. They could rent a house. But he'd have to get a full-time job to help pay for it. Then they'd have to put Baxter in daycare, and he'd have to work more to help pay for that. For now, they're happy in two bedrooms with a killer view, taking advantage of the urban opportunities for kids.

"I would love for him to have a yard," Aaron says. "I loved growing up in suburbia. But that didn't stop me from, once I turned sixteen, wanting to get the hell out and live in a city and wanting to walk everywhere. I would love to have seen (the city) when I was a kid."

Jessixa and Aaron's Baxter juggle reminds me of something I heard Dr. Phil say (and, seriously, this is my only Dr. Phil reference, and it's not that I watch Dr. Phil, but I saw a YouTube clip of him interviewing the swaddle/shushing master, Dr. Karp, in which he said this, so . . .): "We have to remember that kids join our life, we don't join theirs."

Rather than completely overhaul the way their family operates, they decided to keep doing what they were doing, and invite Baxter to participate.

"There was no huge discussion," Aaron says. "It was just kind of, like, welcome to the family."

The Todd and Jamie Method, Part II

The nice thing about Jamie's job as a hairstylist is that she's self-employed and can set her own schedule. The downside is that she's self-employed and can set her own schedule.

"Sometimes I overwork myself because I can," she says. "And sometimes I end up not working as much as I need."

When she was pregnant with Townes, she planned on taking eight weeks off work. Self-employment doesn't come with maternity leave, so she had to save up cash for every day she'd be away from her shears. The plan was for a natural birth, followed by two months off at home with her baby, while Todd worked during the day as a web developer at Third Man Records in Nashville.

It didn't work out that way.

To start with, Townes was three weeks late. And when you're a hairdresser and blocked out eight weeks to not see clients, it's not like you can just keep working up until the day the baby's born. Then, she had to have a C-section, so the natural birth went right out the window.

Since Townes was born so late, she didn't get to stay home with him as long as she'd planned, so they jumped into their childcare juggle a few weeks early. Here's how the week looks.

Sunday: The whole family's home together.

Monday: Todd's at work, Jamie's at home with Townes.

Tuesday: Todd and Jamie both work, and Townes spends the day with Jamie's mom, who lives across the street. Jamie pumped breast milk at work for the first year of his life.

Wednesday: Todd and Jamie work while Townes hangs out with a family friend. Townes subsisted largely on breast milk, but because he's such a big kid, they supplemented with formula and he ate both like a champ.

Thursday: Todd and Jamie both work, and Townes spends another day with Jamie's mom.

Friday: Todd's at work, Jamie's at home with Townes.

Saturday: Jamie's cutting hair, and Townes and Todd do guy things. They watch football and basketball, get tacos together, and then get outside and play sports. "It's just bro-down day," Todd says. "We also go to the park a lot or we'll go play baseball, just me and him."

I can attest to how much fun it is to play sports with a child who can't walk and can barely stay upright—and of the benefit of a planned day or half day alone with a newborn. If you're not the one who's home alone the most with a child, it gives you a much better understanding of what it's like to be on baby duty for an entire day, and how taxing it is in ways you've never felt. It also gives you a fresh look at who your baby is, not just in the hours that you're home, but throughout the arc of his day. If you can swing it, try running point for an entire week. It's illuminating.

When Thomas was two, we got a call one morning from Betsy's sister informing us that their dad had been diagnosed with cancer. She flew home later that day and was gone for a week. Yes, the childcare juggle never stops, and is always changing. Especially when there's a crisis.

This happened when I was still working in an office, so, fortunately, my mom was available to watch Thomas for a couple of afternoons after daycare, and I talked my bosses into letting me work from home the other days.

I'd spent a couple days—OK, maybe thirty-six hours—alone with Thomas before, and I knew I had all the tools to keep up with him, but I didn't know what it would feel like.

The most superficial way to describe it would be "exhausting." But it was tiring in the way that a long run or a good swim in the pool is taxing, in a way that makes you feel better.

Being alone with me for a week was a big adjustment for Thomas, too. And I picked up this vibe from him that we were both in it together, and that we were both getting to know each other a little better. I was there to take him out of bed every morning, drive him to school, feed him, keep him entertained when he got home, and put him in bed when he was tired. He got to see me through the whole day, too, what I was like first thing in the morning without any help, and the things I did to get through the day.

We ate a lot of potatoes and Burger King ice-cream cones. We ate the spuds because I realized I could get a cheap bag of them at Costco, then bake six or seven at a time that could be easily reheated in the microwave for a quick snack (for both of us) or meal (yes, both of us) on the fly. The ice-cream cones were perfect because it was the summer, BK was selling them for less than a buck, and there are few things that lifts a kid's spirits (especially when he's been away from his mom for a few days) more than some soft-serve.

When Betsy got back, I was excited to see her, but I wasn't exactly excited to share all the little things yet. I missed being the one he relied on completely to make him his breakfast and to read him books and to be the person he came scampering to when he woke up in the middle of the night.

Bonding with children is real, something I recognized immediately after Lucy was born. Our connection felt different at first. Thinner, perhaps. It wasn't that I loved her any less than Thomas, but there wasn't the bond that Thomas and I had built together. It takes time.

Bonding is what's happening between dudes like Todd and Townes when they feed the ducks, find themselves tacos, and watch football on a Saturday afternoon. That Townes doesn't yet know the difference between tripe and tongue, quarterback and quarter pounder is of no importance.

Week 23

You Can Do Better, Even If You've Never Seen It Done Before

Your baby weighs about a pound.

Your lady is experiencing mood swings.

The situation: You didn't have a strong fatherhood role model and are worried you won't be able to pull it off.

The reality: It's normal to have doubts. But if you've gotten to week twenty-three in a baby book, you're either extremely creepy or you want to be a great dad. Not that you have to read books to be a great dad, I'm just saying that if you got this far, you mean to do well.

I've never seen my friend Tyler in the shower. So, naturally, I was all ears when his wife walked me through one of her husband's scrub sessions that got a little louder than normal.

"I was woken up to the sounds of him sobbing," Chelsea told me. "Not just crying, sobbing."

Tyler gets up at four o'clock every morning. By the time you're smelling the grounds work their way through the percolator, he's a third of the way into a ten-hour shift. He's always been this way.

I've never known Tyler to be without a job. In high school, he bagged groceries and tossed pizza dough. In college, he worked the door at one of the nicest hotels in Seattle. He's the one who told me that Paul Simon and Prince have the same request on their tour rider: hotel employees are not to look them in the eyes.

Like the rest of us, Tyler drank a bit too much at football games on Saturday afternoons during college. Unlike the rest of us, afterward he helped himself to a sponge bath and a cup of coffee and put in a full shift at work. He's always done well, too. After breakfast with our better halves during one of our last years in school, we were walking down the street and, approaching a sparkling Audi, I joked: "Is this yours?"

Yes.

After college, he continued doing well. Chelsea, too. He appraised buildings. She spoke on behalf of a large tech company that you've heard of. They bought a nice house in a good neighborhood. They got a husky named Denali. They love that dog.

They hated their jobs.

It's not just that the hours were long and the commute was a drag: work didn't make them happy. And they wanted to have kids. They had an idea of the kind of lives they wanted to live with their kids and, more specifically, the kind of care they wanted to provide them. They decided that there were two ways to do it: work a lot, and pay someone else to help them raise their family; or be away from home less and handle more of it themselves. The latter wasn't possible with their jobs and commutes.

Then Tyler began to make wine.

He took a couple classes at a local community college at night, and filled a plastic bucket in his man cave with grapes and watched them ferment. Then the real estate market collapsed and he got the dreaded call to the boss' office.

At first, they were petrified. Chelsea left work early and they spent the rest of the day at the bar. By the time they got home, they had a plan: they were going to move to Walla Walla, the heart of Washington state's wine country and, you know, get into the wine business. Or something.

Tyler did his homework and realized that since his industry was in the shitter the state would pay for him to get retrained in something more practical—like making Syrah. So, he enrolled at the winemaking program at Walla Walla Community College. They rented out their home in Seattle. Chelsea took a job (and pay cut) at a local university and spent a few months freelancing for the man on the side.

A few years later, Chelsea had a job handling marketing for a winery that fills bottles you've seen at Whole Foods. And Tyler crushed grapes at a nearby vineyard when he wasn't sobbing in the shower.

"It was a week before Ollie was born," Chelsea told me about the shower incident. "Tyler was exhausted from long harvest hours, and it was starting to sink in that this little human was going to be here and he panicked that he never had a good example of what it means to be a dad and how could he possibly be a good father. He lost it."

Tyler was raised, more or less, by his mom and stepfather, a general contractor who worked seven days a week. There were a lot of expenses: a nice house, a boat, and three kids to feed. He was around, Tyler told me, but never really there. Worse, Tyler never felt like he knew if the guy he called dad really cared.

"I knew he did," he told me, "but I had to wonder."

Tyler didn't ever want his kids to have to wonder. Instead of giving them a boat, he was going to give them all the time he could. So, when Tyler was offered the chance to run the wine-making operations at a winery, he figured out that he could do the job that he loved and raise his kids the way he wanted to, but there was a catch: he had to work four tens. Not only was it better for his family, it was better for business. It takes a lot of time to set up and tear down a winemaking operation for a day. Working four long days meant fewer hours spent not making wine during the week, and more productivity.

Later, when Tyler was offered the top winemaking job at a winery an hour outside of town, he kept up the four-day work-week and started getting up at four. No, getting up at four doesn't get easier, but he didn't want to sacrifice his day off with the kids.

It's worked out well. They now have a second child, Charlotte, and he has the two of them all to himself every Friday. Last winter he took Ollie skiing every week.

The job's not perfect. During the harvest, weeks go by where he rarely sees his kids.

"Being there doesn't mean being there all the time, but being there when it matters," he says. "If you're asking the question—am I going to be a good dad?—you're going to be just fine, because it means you care."

As far as I know, Scott Coltrane's run-up to fatherhood didn't include mornings in the shower crying in the fetal position, but the noted sociologist, who recently wrapped up a year as the interim president of the University of Oregon, was in a similar position to Tyler when he found out he was going to become a dad in the seventies. He didn't have a great fatherhood role model in his life growing up, and he wanted to know how to be one. So, he read everything he could get his hands on and went back to school.

Coltrane already had a degree and was working as a city planner, but to learn more about kids he enrolled in some child-development classes at a local community college. Then he took a part-time job at an after-school daycare and joined some parenting groups. Sometimes he was the only dad in the bunch. As he was picking up tips on how to be a dad, he realized that he could look beyond men for parenting role models.

"[There] wasn't like a guy way to do it and a woman, motherly way to do it," he says. "There was just parenting and you learn from the people who can do it and that [was] mostly women."

After his kids were born, he started looking for ways that he could better balance his family and career. He decided to indulge his interest in parenting—particularly the role of fathers—and go back to grad school and study sociology. Like my friend Tyler, he had an idea of the kind of father he wanted to be and went back to school and changed careers to pay for it. He has been studying fatherhood, masculinity, gender roles, and paternity leave ever since.

"One of the most enriching experiences that a man can have and one of the most emotionally rewarding experiences is to be an involved parent, and an involved partner," he says. "The part that I found very interesting in talking to young parents is that men aren't trained as boys to either take care of their partners or their kids. And part of the beauty of the dailyness of parenting is that men learn how to serve other people in a way that is quite enriching and probably redresses some of the cultural masculinity mystique."

Parenting—caring for a helpless child—he says, takes practice. Whether men have a positive father figure to look up to or not, none of them have parented until they've become parents. In that regard, we're all starting at the same place.

"Mothers," he said, "don't know how to do it automatically either."

A way to practice for taking care of a kid, Coltrane says, is to take care of a pregnant woman. In a way, your relationship with the two is very similar: they're both people you love, people you're in the same room with and responsible for taking care of. But all the changes are happening to their bodies, not yours (anxiety-inducing weight gain notwithstanding). You don't know what your wife feels like any more than you know what it feels like to be six days old.

"You are estranged from the process," Coltrane says, "and so you have to get aligned with your partner as a precursor to what it's like to serve your kids."

Not that anyone is suggesting telling your wife that she's the guinea pig, but . . .

week 24

You Can't Properly Install a Car Seat Unless You've Seen It Done Before

Your baby has a face, and it's filling out.

Your lady is experiencing backaches. You know what to do.

The situation: Your shopping list is getting long and expensive.

The reality: No, you're not letting down your child by going cheap once in a while. But spend wisely.

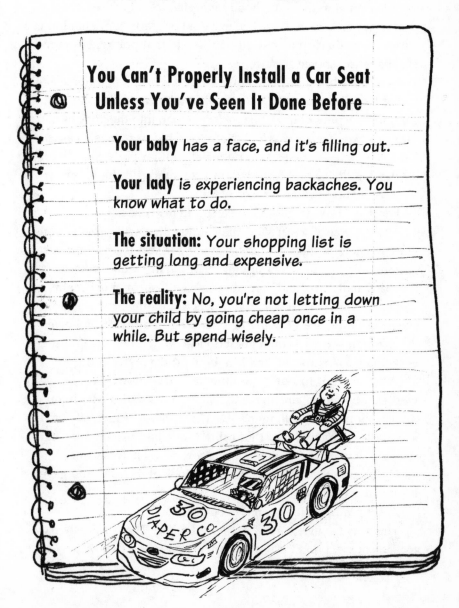

I've always been a little smug about my car-seat skills. Next to swaddling, installing a rear-facing car seat is one of the most enjoyable events in the fatherhood olympics. Infant car seats really aren't supposed to move. When installed properly, they shouldn't budge more than an inch. Getting them to that point takes practice, patience, and endurance.

Before we brought Lucy home from the hospital, a nurse escorted us to our car to make sure we had a car seat installed (a common hospital policy). She took one look into the back of our Camry, saw what she was looking for, and bid us farewell. I asked her to check it—to make sure I'd installed it properly. She held it by the handle, gave it a push, and pronounced it the finest car-seat installation she'd ever seen.

For this, I have to give all the credit to my coach, Norm.

There are services around the country that will provide you with someone to help you install your car seat (ask about local options at your next OB appointment). They don't take long, they're usually free, and they can come with surprising benefits.

Before we went to our first-timers appointment, I was a bit skeptical of the need for any help, and figured that if I followed the directions to a T I could get it done. I went down the line, did everything as instructed, and I thought I did a pretty good job.

When we got to our appointment in downtown Seattle, we were met by Norm, an energetic fellow in his sixties who immediately slipped into calling me "Dad" and Betsy "Mom." Before I let him tell me anything, I told him that I had installed the car seat and wanted him to give me a report card. He was game.

He opened the back door, took one look at the seat, and gave the belt a gentle pull.

"Well, Dad, this looks pretty good . . . "

This was his nice way of saying I'd failed. That's actually par for the course. I don't care who you are, you don't know how to install a car seat. When the National Highway Traffic Safety Administration conducted a study to see what percentage of users could install their car seats properly, between 95 and 100 percent of users made at least one error, depending on the type of seat.

Me? Yeah, I'd gotten the seat into the car. Yes, I'd pulled the seatbelt into the buckle. But I'd forgotten to pull the belt all the way out so that it would catch, and then tighten it against the seat so that it couldn't move.

I know, that doesn't make any sense, does it? That's why you need to have someone show you how to install your car seat. Plus, you might get the chance to meet someone like Norm.

While Norm was giving us his spiel, he told us that, in 1973, he was the first father to stay with his wife as she gave birth at the hospital where his son, John, was born.

I tracked him down five years later. I wanted to hear the whole story about being a fatherhood pioneer.

To start, I wanted to know how he made it happen. It's a short story.

"I just asked," he told me. "Our doctor was quite progressive, I think, for his time, and I asked whether I could be in the delivery room and he said, 'Well I don't see why not.'"

The nurses weren't nearly as accommodating. They were certain that he was going to pass out, and be little more than a lump on the floor for them to deal with while they received his son. But they had Norm all wrong. This wasn't his first rodeo.

"I grew up around a farm. I attended the birth of many calves and had to assist in a couple of those kinds of things, so I knew what was gonna happen and that it wasn't the prettiest of sights. That didn't deter me. I mean, this was my son."

But he didn't know that it was his son. This was 1973. They had no idea what he was getting until the doctor handed him his crying child.

"And the thrill of holding your newborn son ten seconds after he was born cannot be described. It was one of the most miraculous things I've ever experienced."

After Norm told me the story about the birth of his son, I asked him whether he had any other children. In fact, he has a daughter. Only he wasn't able to witness her birth, much as he would have liked to.

A couple years after John was born, Norm and his wife decided to adopt a child from South Korea as something of a tribute to Norm's brother, John, who went missing in action in Korea in 1950.

"My wife and I decided that a good way to honor the memory of my brother and all the other men who perished in that conflict would be to offer a loving home to a child who otherwise wouldn't have such a thing."

When Norm told his mother of their plans, she was quite upset. He remembers her asking, "Well, why do you want one of *them*? They killed your brother."

Though they told the adoption agency that they'd be open to adopting an older child, the agency sent them a picture of an infant who had been found in a garbage heap when she was less than a day old. "It took us all of two nanoseconds to say yes."

Before Norm and his wife went to the airport to pick up their daughter, Norm called his mom and asked her whether she wanted to come along. She grumbled about it, but ultimately agreed to get in the car.

Their daughter flew with an escort on a Pan Am flight from Seoul to Honolulu, and Honolulu to Seattle. They had been told in advance to have skim milk and rice cereal ready for her. After every other passenger had exited the plane, their little girl, now nine months old, emerged from the Boeing 747 in the arms of her escort, saw Norm's wife with the milk, and "almost jumped from the escort's arms into my wife's arms."

"I turned to my mom and said, 'Do you want to hold your granddaughter?' And a lot of healing happened in a very short period of time. She took Ruth in her arms and you could not have pried her out with a crowbar."

I like Norm's stories because I like the idea of dads and parents doing things that they've never seen done before and that other people think is a bad idea. I don't claim to have broken any barriers, but I've always thought tradition and habit were two of the worst justifications for our actions.

Pregnancy and child-rearing are rife with tradition, handed down via our childhood memories and unsolicited advice. When you and your lady want to break the mold and do something that's best for your family, even if it's never been done before, go for it. Do what Norm did. Make it happen.

And make sure you properly install your car seat.

Consider the Formula

Your baby is already growing adult teeth.

Your lady is being frightened into breast-feeding, no matter what.

The situation: You are willing to take turns feeding in the middle of the night.

The reality: Formula feeding is a safe, healthy option, and may be best for your family. Seriously, weigh the pros and cons. And ask your doctor.

Even though we'd been through a birth before and were, you know, so educated on the ways of pregnancy and childbirth that one of us was writing a book on the topic, we took the hospital tour again before Lucy was born because she was coming into this world at a different hospital than Thomas.

Aside from learning where to park, what the birthing "suites" look like, and what to order off the menu, the tour is a good chance to get preregistration paperwork out of the way early and assess hospital policies. This hospital, for example, allowed up to five guests in the room at a time, and each guest had to wear a paper tag bearing the room number clipped to their shirt. No big deal. Betsy wasn't hoping for a large crowd.

The registered nurse who gave us our tour was pleasant enough. But when I asked if there would be baby formula at the ready in the room, you could hear the record come to a screeching halt. There would not, she said, be any formula in the room. Formula, she informed us, was considered a form of treatment, and in order to get some we'd have to get an OK from Betsy's doctor.

This didn't land well.

"Wait," I said. "So, you're telling me that we have to ask for permission to give our daughter formula?"

"Well," she said. "It's considered treatment, so you have to ask the doctor for it. But let's ask the lactation consultants."

"OK," I said. "That's fine. I just need to know whether I need to bring formula with me to the hospital, because I don't need permission to feed my daughter."

A couple minutes later we found a door with a sticker explaining that a mother's breast serves all your baby's needs. Breast-feeding propaganda is rampant among habitats in which pregnant women are known to traverse. A nurse stuck her head out the door and our tour guide/registered nurse asked the other nurse whether we had to ask for permission to give our daughter baby formula.

"No," she said. "All you have to do is ask for it and we'll bring it over."

The scary thing is that this medical professional charged with giving parents the lowdown on the first day of their child's life could get this so wrong. But it's a good example of how much misinformation is spread in the breast-feeding versus formula conversation—not that it's really a conversation. It's more like a campaign of guilt and shame in the battle of how women should choose, brought on by people who are otherwise inclined to stand up against wars of guilt and shame in the battle of how women should choose.

Betsy considered breast-feeding for round two, but she put down some stipulations. To start, she wasn't going to let her daughter live her first few days in abundant stress, bouncing from lactation consultant to support group between midnight feedings of drips of colostrum. If it worked, it worked. But she wasn't going to put herself or her newborn child through what happened the first time.

* * *

I've told you a lot about Thomas, but I don't think I've done enough boasting. I'm sure your child is going to be special and beautiful in her own little way, but, damn, Thomas is off the charts. Literally. Since the day he was born he's been off the charts in height, and he's well above average for weight—enough to be strong, but, you know, not an overweight child. (I've been off the charts my whole life, too, but at a certain point the doctor stopped congratulating my parents for it.)

Thomas helps clean the grill and take care of his sister. He helps Betsy bake cookies and play Bejeweled. He knows how to hack into the Netflix app on my phone and call up his favorite show—whatever it is that week. He's not yet five, but he's already writing notes and placing them on his mother's pillow while she sleeps.

This is all the more incredible when you consider that he's accomplished all this—and at such an early age—in spite of his troubled upbringing. Thomas [insert painful silence here] grew up on formula.

Betsy had every intention of breast-feeding Thomas, and we both listened intently as the doula leading our six-week pregnancy course talked about the virtues of breast-feeding, what to do if you're having trouble breast-feeding, and what buses to take to find the lactation consultant so that she, like the American Academy of Pediatrics suggests, can "exclusively breast-feed for about six months." But there was no mention of the benefits associated with formula—only that the stuff was expensive, and didn't help mothers lose weight like feeding off the breast does.

Betsy really wanted to breast-feed. She tried. Really hard. But it wasn't easy, if it ever is. There were problems with the "latch" and with Thomas getting enough to eat. We went to the consultant, rented a pump, and were up every two hours for a hazy routine of turning on the machine, attaching the tubes, applying the supplemental nipple system, and trying to feed a crying baby. There wasn't much milk, but there were plenty of tears.

Begrudgingly, we gave up and bought the Costco pack of Enfamil. We brought it home, shook up a batch, and noticed the comforting words placed prominently across the front of the box: "Experts agree, breast-feeding is best." Thanks. We needed that. Betsy really needed it. She already thought she'd failed, that she somehow didn't produce for her son when he needed her most.

Thomas has always been a good sleeper (he excels at everything, remember?) and when he was an infant he was kind enough to go at least three hours between meals. So when Betsy

was breast-feeding, that meant we *only* had to get up every couple hours to heat up the pump, and try to extract a few drops before his second midnight snack. Some friends had it much worse.
One baby in our circle needed to be fed every hour. To give her
child the "ideal," his mom didn't sleep for days.

When we switched to formula, everything changed. Only one
of us had to get up. That meant that I could get up on my own
and feed Thomas while his mom stayed in bed for six straight
hours of sleep. (I tell you what, at 3 a.m., that "breast-feeding is
best" label may as well have said "wake up that lazy mother and
make her do it herself!")

The advantages extended beyond quality REM sleep. I got to
bond with Thomas. I got to sing him songs and tell him stories. I
got to take him to my parents' house for the day—without worry-
ing about having enough milk or keeping it cold—and give Betsy
an afternoon to rest.

But men feeding infants, and infants feeding off of anything
but mom's nipple, is anathema to the most vocal constituency of
the "breast is best" wing of the medical establishment and their
hangers-on. For example, during one of our birthing classes, I
made the mistake of suggesting that I help feed our newborn.

> **Me:** So, since the baby is going to need to feed every two or
> three hours, can't she pump so that we can trade off getting up
> in the night? That way we'd each get a four- or five-hour
> stretch of sleep each night?
> **Doula:** Now, why would she be pumping?

I'm not kidding. The scary thing is that this doula is not alone.
Even women who feed their children breast milk from a bottle
are considered failures. One of our friends was shamed to tears
when she couldn't keep up feeding on the boob and started feeding her son pumped breast milk.

Telling a mom today—when the majority of women are working outside of the home—that she shouldn't be pumping, that she shouldn't be feeding her child formula, that she should take six months off of work to feed her child, isn't just unreasonable, it's irresponsible.

Dr. Judy Kimelman, the obstetrician in Seattle I mentioned earlier, told me the message to women shouldn't be that they *have* to breast-feed. Rather, she advocates for encouraging women to try as hard as they can, and if breast-feeding doesn't work out, it's OK because there are good alternatives.

"There's no question that there's so much pressure on women to breast-feed, that if they're unable it just adds so much anxiety and sense of failure," she told me. "Sometimes I feel like my job is to give women permission to say, 'I just can't do it.' Instead of, 'You know, let's try this, let's try more,' because they've already done that to themselves."

A 2014 study of mothers in the United Kingdom showed that women at the highest risk for postpartum depression were the ones who had planned to breast-feed but were unable to. They were more than twice as likely to get depressed than women who never planned to breast-feed and didn't breast-feed.

This is consistent with something Betsy's OB told us during an appointment. She said she's seen an uptick in women developing postpartum depression when they're unable to breast-feed. When Betsy told the doctor she was considering feeding Lucy formula, the doc encouraged her to feel good about her decision. She has three children herself, and after breast-feeding the first two, she decided to formula-feed the third. Because she wasn't stressed out about the logistics of juggling two kids and a job while feeding her third baby on the boob, she felt much more relaxed, and free to bond with her child.

These are benefits you're not likely to hear from lactation consultants and their ilk.

* * *

To our surprise and delight, Lucy took to the breast in the hospital. And for a while, it looked like things were going to work out
this time. But they didn't.

Once again, Betsy put herself through the unproductive 2 a.m.
feedings, the pumping, the stress of caring for an underfed baby,
and literature that told her she wasn't giving her child the best
life possible.

One morning we stopped in to see a lactation consultant
during a community drop-in time—which are phenomenal resources. Before we could see the consultant, we had to endure a
few more pieces of breast-feeding propaganda. Two of my favor-
ites: the "Affordable Health Care Starts With Breast-feeding"
bumper sticker and the "Breast-feeding Is the Best Thing In the
World" poster that features pictures of happy families and nurs-
ing mothers from all over the world.

Behind the counter, a greasy-haired breast-feeding activist
with a radar for mothers who were considering formula had her
fangs out. She gave Betsy her spiel for how to avoid pumping.
Next door, the consultant's message was completely different.

She was, obviously, a breast-feeding advocate, and was happy
to help us any way she could. But she didn't try to scare Betsy
into breast-feeding. She encouraged us to do what was right for
the family. Unfortunately, I've still never seen a sticker or poster
in a hospital or clinic that said: "Bottle or Breast: You Decide
What's Best!"

So, that's what we decided to do. We stocked up on formula
and watched Lucy grow. She is, of course, uncommonly smart,
strong, and beautiful—just like her mother. At eight months old,
it's hard to tell which Ivy League school she's going to attend, but
it will be nice to have options.

You, too, have options.

I'm not trying to convince you to feed your baby one way or
the other, just like I'm not trying to convince you to raise your

baby a specific way or to hammer out a prescribed work/life balance. I think families should make informed decisions, and feel good about making the decisions that are right for them, and I think they should be made from a place of strength, not guilt and shame.

While I was researching this issue, I called up Dr. Joan Meek, the chair of the American Academy of Pediatrics's section on breast-feeding. She told me more than a few things that I found interesting.

"I think if a woman has been given the appropriate information and makes the decision that it's not for her, that she's going to formula-feed, then I think she should be supported in that decision as well," she told me. "[Breast-feeding] shouldn't be pressured."

That said, she doesn't think it's like flipping a coin. "I do think that from the public health standpoint, we need to be very sort of strong about the message to make sure that women understand it does make a difference. What they ultimately choose to do is their choice. And they accept that risk—and there is some risk—for their own health and for their children."

When I asked her if those differences should be considered "modest," as studies often suggest, she said the problem is that the studies aren't very good.

"We still don't have a lot of great literature that clearly looks at exclusive breast-feeding according to the public health recommendations, which is preferably for about six months only breast-feeding," she told me. "To really have good science, you have to compare that cohort that really followed those recommendations to an exclusively formula-fed group and then really stratify, if they're in-between, exactly how much breast-feeding did they do. And I would suggest that if we had studies that really distinguished that, it would be more helpful."

So, yeah, take everything you've heard about studies that show the benefits of breast-feeding with a grain of salt. Because if the head of the American Academy of Pediatrics's section on breast-feeding doesn't think the science is a slam dunk, perhaps you shouldn't either.

With that in mind, here's a look at a few of the details and rebuttals behind the "breast is best" movement to consider while your family makes its decision.

Claim: Breast-feeding will reduce your baby's risk of gastrointestinal infections!

The World Health Organization recommends exclusive breast-feeding for the first six months of life because it believes that it provides many benefits to mother and baby. "Chief among these," WHO says on its website, "is protection against gastrointestinal infections which is observed not only in developing but also industrialized countries." That sounds really bad. But do you even know what a gastrointestinal infection is? Let's start there.

In a 2001 study published in the *Journal of the American Medical Association* (*JAMA*), the criteria for gastrointestinal infections was two days of at least two of the following symptoms: "increased stool frequency, loose stools, vomiting, and temperature greater than 38.5°C." In plain terms, the study demonstrated that among children of mothers who spent less time breast-feeding, four out of one hundred experienced one additional case of diarrhea or vomiting.

A Dutch study that's cited in the AAP's statement on breast-feeding compared exclusively breast-fed infants with those who had never been breast-fed, which sounds like the kind of study Dr. Meek is looking for. They concluded that yes, a few babies for every hundred missed a bout of diarrhea (etc.) among children who had been breast-fed rather than bottle-fed. But not *all* groups of babies who had been breast-fed saw a benefit over formula-fed babies. In fact, only babies who had been exclusively breast-fed for four months—and partially thereafter—saw any benefit. Curiously, there were no statistically significant lower risks among babies who had been exclusively breast-fed for six months (as the AAP recommends), seven months, or twelve months, compared to those who hadn't been breast-fed at all.

Keep in mind, WHO says reducing the risk of gastrointestinal infection is the "chief" benefit of breast-feeding. In developed nations with clean water, you're looking at, maybe, a missed bout of diarrhea. Or, maybe not.

Claim: Breast-feeding reduces the risk of childhood obesity!

Maybe. Maybe not. The authors of a 2001 study published in JAMA note that "there was no significant reduction in being overweight with being ever breast-fed." The biggest predictor of a child's body mass index, the study found, is its parents. "Risk of overweight among young children was nearly tripled with maternal overweight and more than quadrupled with mothers' obesity."

Claim: Babies who breast-feed have fewer ear infections!

Possibly.

David Meyers, director at the Center for Primary Care at the Agency for Health Care Research and Quality, put the benefits this way in 2009: "The evidence suggests that for every six children who are breast-fed exclusively for the first six months of life, one of them will not have an ear infection that he or she would otherwise have had."

So, there you go. If your wife exclusively breast-feeds six kids, one of them might avoid an ear infection.

Claim: Breast-feeding allows you to cuddle and bond with your baby!

Or, as the AAP puts it at the top of their first breast-feeding page (though not their formula page): "Feeding your infant provides more than just good nutrition. It also gives you a chance to hold your newborn close, cuddle him, and make eye contact. These are relaxing and enjoyable moments for you both, and they bring you closer together emotionally."

But here's the thing: I just held a baby close, cuddled her, made eye contact, and fed her. And I'll be damned if I didn't emotionally connect with her. And I did it without lactating.

Breast-feeding does not have a monopoly on snuggling and making eye contact while feeding.

Claim: Breast-feeding reduces a woman's risk of getting breast cancer!

OK, let's put it in perspective.

Susan G. Komen for the Cure puts the risk of women in the United States getting breast cancer in their lifetime at one in eight, or 12 percent. On its website, Komen cites a study that shows that "mothers who breast-fed for a lifetime total (combined duration of breast-feeding for all children) of one year were slightly less likely to get breast cancer than those who never breast-fed." The study shows that a woman's risk drops by 4.3 percent. That means that if a woman breast-feeds for a year, she's still in the one in eight neighborhood.

It's worth noting that the same study showed that a woman's risk of developing breast cancer drops by 7 percent just by giving birth. Additionally, Komen says that "women who give birth for the first time after age 35 are 40 percent more likely to get breast cancer than women who have their first child before age 20."

Hopefully nobody's recommending teenagers get pregnant to avoid breast cancer.

Claim: Formula-feeding is more expensive than breast-feeding!

OK, this is the worst of all, and it's trotted out repeatedly by people who should know better. Breast-feeding is only cheaper than formula-feeding if you also believe that it saves money for children to stay home with their mothers as opposed to going to daycare. In her brilliant piece in the *Atlantic*, "The Case Against Breast-Feeding," Hanna Rosin puts the cost of breast-feeding this way: "It's only free if a woman's time is worth nothing." If a woman is going to exclusively feed on the breast for six months, as the AAP recommends, she's not going to be working outside the home. And even if she's pumping, she's going to be taking time out of work to express milk. Plus, when you're self-employed, like I am, and your wife has trouble breast-feeding, it becomes immediately clear that it saps both of you of money-earning productivity. I'm not saying that people shouldn't breast-feed because it's too expensive. All I'm saying is that formula-feeding is *not more expensive* than breast-feeding.

Claim: Breast-feeding protects your baby against SIDS, asthma, and other kinds of nasty things!

Not necessarily.

The AAP says: "Research also suggests that breast-feeding may help to protect against obesity, diabetes, sudden infant death syndrome (SIDS), asthma, eczema, colitis, and some cancers." Yes, some studies do suggest that it does. Other studies suggest that it does not. Why the discrepancy? Nobody really knows. But

one common problem with breast-feeding studies was acknowl-
edged in an article that Dr. Meek sent me:

"One of the well-known confounders in breast-feeding research
is demographic difference between mothers who breast-feed and
those who chose not to breast-feed due to self-selection . . . mothers
who breast-feed tend to be white (versus non-Hispanic black or
African American), older, more educated, and in a higher socioeco-
nomic stratum."

In other words: women who breast-feed are often richer (they
can afford to miss work to feed on the breast), older, and better
educated than women who formula-feed. Studies try to control
for this, but it's still hard to tell if studies that show benefits of
breast-feeding are really showing the benefits of affluence.

Rather than just compare breast-fed babies to formula-fed babies, Cynthia G. Colen and David M. Ramey compared children
who had been breast-fed with siblings who had been formula-
fed. This is interesting because you're looking at outcomes from
the same family: the same race, income bracket, neighborhood,
parents, etc. They found that not only are there not significant differences in four- to fourteen-year-olds who had been breast-fed
versus siblings who were formula-fed, but that "for some outcomes, breast-fed children may actually be worse off than children who were not breast-fed." For example, their study
suggested that children who are breast-fed may actually be at a
higher risk for asthma than siblings who were formula-fed.

When I spoke to Dr. Colen about her study, she told me that it
would be a mistake to come away thinking there are no benefits
to breast-feeding.

"I think breast-feeding is wonderful. I think it's beneficial. I
think it can help, for many different reasons—it can be very convenient," she told me. "But I think we have to have a more nuanced
discussion and we have to trust women more to consume the
health information around breast-feeding, rather than 'it's a black

and white issue: you're good if you do it, you're bad if you don't.' In not presenting the entire picture to women, I think we are selling women short in terms of what they can understand and how they view the benefits and drawbacks of breast-feeding."

Yes, there are probably some benefits to breast-feeding. Yes, they're probably modest. No, you're not setting your child back in the long run if you choose to feed him formula.

Week 26

Pick a Pediatrician You Actually Like

Your baby has developed all five senses.

Your lady wants you to go see the doctor.

The situation: It's about time for you to pick a doctor for the baby.

The reality: You could stand to find a regular doc, too.

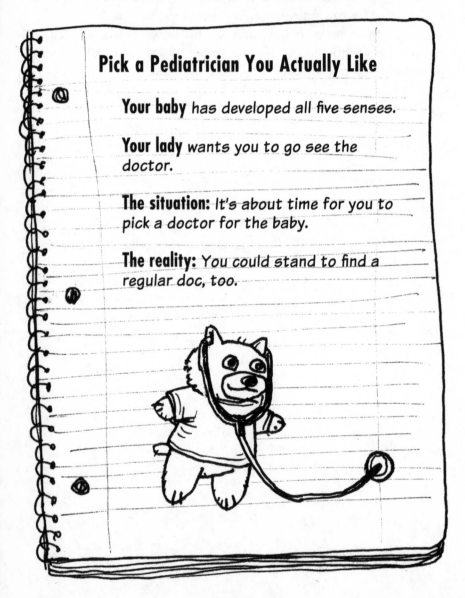

I don't know about you, but I've never picked a doctor for my- self. Going to see the doctor hasn't been much different than go- ing to see the principal: it's usually been because I screwed up. I never had any say in the matter.

When I was a kid, I went to see Dr. Keyes, and I guarantee you my parents didn't seek my opinion on the subject. He was just "the doctor," and I had no more say in the matter than I did who delivered the mail or hauled away our trash.

Once I got older and was given employer-provided health in- surance, Betsy suggested that I go see my doctor, even though there was nothing wrong with me—and I didn't even have a doc- tor. "Why am I going to the doctor?" I wanted to know. "Because you haven't gone in four or five years!" she said.

Some people get really hung up on their doctor, like it's some kind of spiritual relationship. During the Affordable Care Act de- bate, the most sinister attacks weren't about death panels or rais- ing rates, they were the ones that suggested that the law would put something—someone! somewhere!—between you and your doctor. This is a problem primarily for first world old people who (a) not only get health care, but get to choose a provider and (b) need to be provided for a lot.

That's not me. But when I couldn't put Betsy off anymore, I called the number on the back of my insurance card and was, mag- ically, given a time to see "my doctor." To be clear, I didn't choose the time, place, or doc, but there I was, sitting in the waiting room.

My doc's nurse blew away every stereotype I'd ever had about the profession: he was big, black, a vet and, as he took my blood pressure, explained that he was the author of multiple ro- mance novels.

"My doc" was sunburned, friendly, and just as confused about why I was in his office as I was. I explained that my wife was on me about not going to see the doctor in four or five years. "You listen to your wife?"

We responded in unison: "Every four or five years."

Babies, it turns out, have to see the doc a bit more often (vaccines, etc.). I'm sure there are people who consult the local city magazine to be sure that they get one of the "125 Best Pediatricians In Town!" But, here's the thing: I've made those lists. I know how they're put together. And I'm not going to leave a serious, life-altering decision to the me at that magazine.

We found our pediatrician on a cardboard sign.

Betsy's OB shared space with a pediatric practice, and one day after we were told we should start shopping around for a doctor for the kid, I noticed a cardboard (or synthetic replacement) sign next to the pediatrician check-in advertising the return of Dr. David Bowe. The doctor, the sign proclaimed, had spent the last year treating children in Tanzania, but was now back and taking patients.

We looked around a bit, we interviewed a couple, but from the start I had a feeling that the doctor who'd just worked with kids in Africa was our guy. Not for any idealistic reasons, of course, but because I assumed that a guy who'd seen families deal with hunger and the HIV epidemic at third-world levels would be a bit levelheaded when it came to doling out dogma and guilt. We were right.

His default position is an assured smile. He didn't come down on us when Betsy started formula feeding. He never came down on us about anything. He smiled and told us Thomas was going to be fine.

We were sad when we moved out of town and had to find a new pediatrician, but I caught up with Dr. Bowe recently to ask him for some tips. Specifically, I was interested in the things parents could do for children early on that would make the most impact. I was anticipating reading or some kind of early education. Nope.

Vaccines.

"That is a huge thing for preventing illness in kids," he told me. "I think that's probably right up there as one of the top things you can do as a parent."

Oddly, in areas of the country like mine (Seattle) where parents are most likely to breast-feed, they're also some of the most likely to skip the immunizations. Don't get me started.

It's easy to get bogged down in the minutia—the pacifier debate, breast versus bottles, am I reading enough to my two-week-old?—but it's the big stuff, the low-hanging fruit (car seats, vaccines, "back is best") that have the most impact.

Find a pediatrician before the baby's born and she—or a member of the team—will probably come check on the baby in the hospital. Find one you like, if you can. If not, just find one.

And if you haven't been to see the doctor in four or five years, it wouldn't kill you to show your doctor that you still care.

week 27

Don't Be Afraid to Be an Asshole

Your baby is the size of an eggplant.

Your lady has swollen ankles.

The situation: You're trying to be there for her at the doctor's appointments.

The reality: The door keeps slamming in your face.

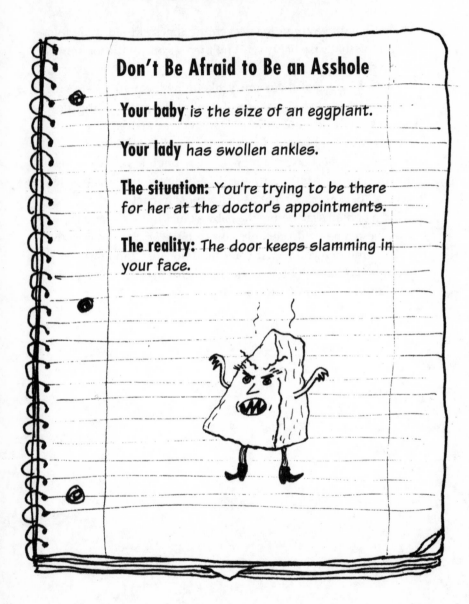

There's no upside for the guy in the "we're pregnant" debate. Saying "my girlfriend's pregnant" is going to get you in deep shit. "Oh, she's pregnant? You're just, what, a bystander?"

Saying "my wife and I are pregnant" is going to get you in deep shit. "Oh, no, no, no, you're not pregnant, too. Are you carrying around a baby?"

Wade into the "we're pregnant" conversation at your own peril, but one thing is clear: when you accompany her to the doctor's office, dad's definitely not pregnant, too. Don't be surprised if you find yourself about as welcomed at the clinic as you would be in the huddle at a roller-derby match.

When I stepped up to the counter with Betsy as she checked in for her first appointment after we got an indication that Lucy was on board, the woman behind the desk—and, yes, they're all women—asked me whether I would step aside so that she could ask Betsy if I had been abusing her. Fair enough. You'll probably get the same. And no matter what she says, you'll be viewed with suspicion for the next eight months.

A few minutes later, another nurse asked Betsy to come back to an examination room. Oh, but, sir, I'm going to have to ask you to wait here. After Betsy returned from answering a few innocuous questions about her medical history, another nurse asked her to come back and didn't tell me to stay behind. Sure, she was a bit cold and didn't say a word to me, but at least I got in the door. And it's important that you do.

Pregnant women have questions. Pregnant women feel things in places they didn't know they had. She's not going to remember all the questions she wanted to ask. And she's not going to remember all the answers. She needs you to help remember the answers—and to demand that you get answers. You may or may not be pregnant, too, but you are definitely your lady's advocate. You've seen it done before.

I swear, this is the only time I'm going to mention *Knocked Up*. I know, I know, but bear with me: there are some truths masked behind the dick jokes in the Judd Apatow flick. The best is the way Seth Rogen becomes Katherine Heigl's manager when it's time for her to go and have her baby. She had a birth plan and it was falling apart. Rogen stepped in to try and make it happen on her behalf, to be her advocate.

The details of their situation aren't too important, but they're instructive: a new doctor came into the picture, and Rogen made sure the doc knew his lady's wishes; the doc wasn't being patient with his lady, and he took the doc to town; when Heigl's sister tried to take over the situation and kick Rogen out of the room, he took her outside and explained what's what.

The reason bands have managers is so that they don't have to be assholes. Women in labor are in the most fragile and emotional condition they'll ever be in and they need someone to take care of everything that they can't. She's got enough on her mind and her pelvis.

If your lady doesn't want her mother in the room when she starts to push, you know what to do. If the doctors and nurses don't notice something or aren't being attentive enough, you've got to be the one to speak up. She can't go out of the room to get help—she's got a catheter and an eager baby.

When Betsy was in the hospital with Thomas, she didn't get out of bed until she was almost discharged. This was because there was a large bag of urine attached to her body. Other moms were up, carrying their babies around, using the bathroom and generally doing what they could to recover from the birth. Betsy kept still.

When I finally informed one of the nurses that Betsy was still connected to the bladder bag, she reacted in surprise: that sort of thing is usually taken care of soon after the birth.

Yeah, thanks.

It's not your job to become friends with the nurses. It's your job to take care of your lady. So, don't ever feel bad about asking stupid questions. You'll be surprised how many stupid questions medical professionals don't know the answer to. For example: who's going to perform the circumcision?

I know there's a movement afoot to do away with male circumcisions, and I'm not going to get in the way of that Thanksgiving discussion. But the fact remains that dudes still get circumcised in this country at regular rates. So, it was a surprise to me that nobody seemed to have any idea who would remove my son's foreskin. They knew who was going to check his hearing and give him his first bath. But not the snipping.

When I brought the circumcision up to Betsy's OB a few weeks before the birth, she didn't have a good answer: sometimes I do it, she said, sometimes someone at the hospital will do it . . . and if it doesn't get done at the hospital, you have to bring the baby back to the clinic a few days later.

There are all kinds of reasons to get the snipping done sooner rather than later, but let's start with the fact that it's not going to become easier with time. Parents have a lot to do in the days and weeks that follow the birth of a child. Making a special trip back to the doctor's office to have a piece of their child's genitals removed is not an appointment they're excited to make. It's not one medical professionals are eager to make, either.

Plus—and I don't want to sound unnecessarily cold here—there are financial reasons to have things taken care of in the hospital. When you start making new appointments, the bills stack up.

Birth day came and we still didn't know who was going to snip the tip. I asked the doctor on duty if she would do the honors, but she balked. So, I turned to just about anybody I could get my hands on, and, to my surprise, nobody had an answer. One of the residents—so new and anxious that she tied her hands in knots as a nervous tick—asked if we'd considered hiring a mohel, a Jewish person trained in such matters. We're not Jewish, but I wish I'd thought of that a few weeks earlier.

In the end, Thomas left the hospital with the same parts he came in with, and we returned two weeks later to rectify the situation. Two medical professionals—not doctors, if you can believe it—took Thomas from our arms (we weren't allowed to witness the procedure), and brought him into an examination room for ten minutes. He returned, whimpering, but a real trooper.

The bill was $500.

Can you see where I made my mistake? I shouldn't have let Betsy get to the hospital without a clear word on who would be performing the circumcision. We're the customers, they're the health-care providers. And if nobody would volunteer for the job the morning after the birth, I should have gently informed the doctor that we wouldn't be leaving the hospital before our son was circumcised.

It's OK to be an asshole.

If that makes you uncomfortable, remember that you're not paying $500 to get the runaround.

Week 28

Walk, Don't Run: Giving Birth Isn't Like It Is On TV

Your baby has crossed the two-pound mark.

Your lady is tasting things differently. Pass her the salt.

The situation: You're thinking about speeding to the hospital with a police escort.

The reality: It's not (usually) like that. You're most likely going to be walking (or driving inside the speed limit).

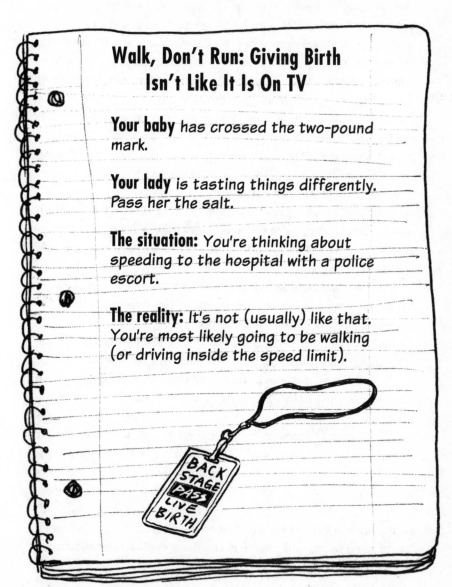

I'm sorry to be the one to tell you this, but her water doesn't always break, there rarely is a high-speed dash to the hospital, and, generally speaking, having a baby isn't like making toast: there is no ding that lets you know the baby's fully cooked.

Giving birth takes a while (usually). There are false starts. There isn't (usually) a clear-cut sign that it's time to go to the hospital. In other words: Hollywood (*Knocked Up* not withstanding) has lied to us all, for a very long time.

This is not for nefarious purposes. It's for your benefit. If Hollywood were to portray the full narrative arc of childbirth, it would be longer than your average miniseries, and few among us want twenty hours of bleeding and groaning (though I maintain that *Shōgun* was not half-bad).

This was all a surprise to me, too, when Betsy was pregnant with Thomas. And, since we lived blocks away from the hospital at which he would be born, I assumed that it meant that we'd be able to save on parking, too.

Contractions are one of the signs a woman's body gives to tell her that her baby is headed for the lobby. But sometimes the baby doesn't take the elevator all the way down.

Eight days after Betsy's due date, she finally started to feel something. She couldn't sleep, she rolled in pain, and she kept track of the rate and length of her contractions. I suggested we walk to the hospital to get things checked out. She handed me my keys.

After Betsy got looked over, we were told that she wasn't far enough along to be admitted. But, perhaps if she went for a walk (like I'd been saying!) it would encourage the baby along. We walked through the hospital for what had to have been a longer stretch than the distance between our home and the birthing suites, then returned for another look. They did their business, found her a room, and twelve hours later, I said hello to Thomas.

I should clarify that "only" the last two of these hours involved Betsy pushing. You see, when a woman is in labor, she's not constantly pushing a baby out. During those two hours, a nurse sat next to Betsy, calmly talking her through what was happening to her body—between sips of coffee from a grande Starbucks cup.

Birth day is the biggest day in any of our lives. You spend months agonizing over every option, opportunity, scenario, and potential shortfall. You read books, watch videos, go to classes.

It's comforting to know that for medical professionals, it's just another day at the office: gossip, coffee, and asshole customers.

* * *

The day before Lucy was due, Betsy started feeling some familiar sensations. The contractions were painful and regular—just a few minutes apart. As we had been instructed to do on such occasions, we called the hospital. Betsy reported her progress, and the nurse on the other end of the line told her to come in. We went into action: we called my mom to come watch Thomas, we grabbed our bags, and we fed the cats.

Betsy stretched out in a hospital bed, and a nurse came in to check her "progress." The nurse did things beneath the sheets that I cared not to witness and the result was something neither of us wanted to hear: the baby would not be born today. Betsy was only a centimeter—actually, more like a fingertip—along. She wasn't even close.

Slightly perturbed, I told the nurse that we'd called ahead and that they said we should come in. "We have to say that," she said. "Just so you know, any time you call, they're going to tell you to come in. Because you never know." She told Betsy she'll know the real contractions when they happen because the pain will be excruciating and she won't be able to walk. Then she sent us both home.

For a woman who's been pregnant for forty weeks, the idea of wrapping things up—of meeting your daughter and having your body back to yourself—is nirvana. Being sent home is a thin slice of hell.

Two days later, activity returned. We knew what would happen if we picked up the phone, so Betsy waited until the pain started to draw tears before we made the call. We told the hospital we were on our way and we told my mom it was time for her to come back. Only, she couldn't come back. Not for another three hours. This, we hadn't planned on.

On the way to the hospital, I scrolled through my phone to see who could toss us a lifeline. Our friend Angela works near the hospital, and was able to get out of work for a couple hours to watch Thomas at the hospital while his mom writhed in pain. I wondered if this was my chance, if I could crank it up to ninety for the ten miles between the house and the hospital. But with a real-life pregnant woman in the seat next to me and a four-year-old in the back, I felt a pang of responsibility, like, maybe not pushing the limits of the Camry we inherited from Betsy's grandma was the safe thing to do.

We waited in a room for what felt like far too long to leave a pregnant woman in constant pain. I flagged down a nurse and asked what the deal was, and why hadn't Betsy been properly checked in yet? "Oh," she said, "I thought that she had." Great, feeling better already!

The nurse did her thing under the sheets and came up with more bad news: just two centimeters. "We usually send people home if they're not at four."

This was too much. Two days ago, Betsy felt discouraged. Now she was devastated. I was sick for her.

A few minutes later, Angela informed me that my mom was waiting in the lobby, but that they wouldn't let her back to the room because they didn't have enough badges. Each patient is allowed up to five guests, but the front desk had somehow misplaced—or the previous tenants had not returned—a couple of the paper visitor badges designated for our room, so they were not letting my mom back to pick up Thomas. Angela said she'd deliver Thomas to my mom, and that it was no big deal. I disagreed.

Popular culture has had a good laugh at the preposterous demands some rock bands put on their tour rider. When Van Halen was at its peak in the eighties, the band's rider noted that no brown M&M's were to be seen backstage. Years later, David Lee Roth said it wasn't that the band were prima donnas (though they were), but that they wanted to know whether the tour promoter had read the rider. They were bringing massive theatrical setups to venues that had never seen anything close. Other elements of the rider included electrical benchmarks and measurements meant to keep their lighting and sound crews safe. If the band went into the dressing room and saw a brown M&M, they knew to look out for other trouble.

Those paper badges were the brown M&M's of the hospital. They'd already forgotten to properly check in Betsy when we arrived, had previously told us we had to ask for permission to feed our daughter formula, and I was trying to juggle a safe situation for Thomas while Betsy wept in pain. The badge was too much.

I informed the front desk that the situation was unacceptable, that we were allowed five guests, that I didn't care that they didn't have enough badges, and that I should have been back in the room with my crying wife, not fucking around with the front desk ensuring that family members could do their business.

Security took issue with that last part, and after I began to cool off I realized I'd let my frustration out on a pair of blue-haired ladies charged with instituting a ridiculous hospital policy. My bad.

At least the badges weren't an issue again.

When I returned to the room, Betsy's condition hadn't improved. The contractions were steady and getting worse. The doctor on call told us she'd check up on Betsy after a couple hours, and during a particularly nasty contraction, I heard a nurse mutter: "Honey, we're not gonna send you home." Miraculously, she moved from two centimeters to five in an hour.

Betsy's water still hadn't broken, but we knew we wouldn't be going home without our baby.

Week 29

You Don't Need a Six-Week Birthing Course (Only a 3x5 Card)

Your baby is up to two and a half pounds.

Your lady may be dealing with varicose veins on her legs. Don't point them out.

The situation: She wants both of you to take a six-week birthing and parenting class.

The reality: A birthing class isn't mandatory. All you really need is a 3x5 notecard.

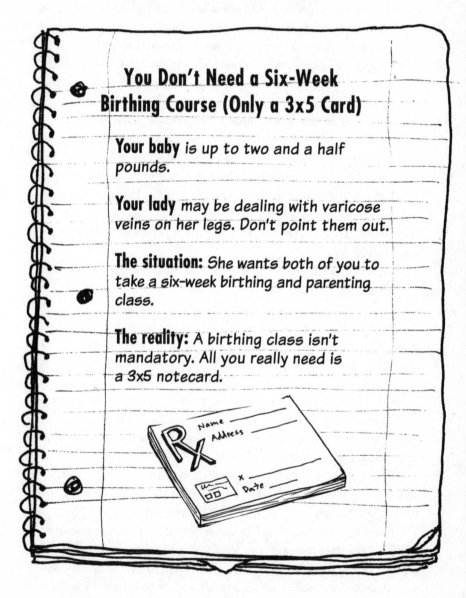

A year before I was born, a young doctor named Greg Keyes, straight out of residency, set up a family practice in a clinic on the island near Seattle where I grew up. He became the doctor of record not only for my brothers and me, but also for many of the area children of my generation, those who straddle the Gen X and Millennial divide, who remember life without the Internet, but not MTV. Three decades later, he's still seeing patients on the same island, and I thought I'd check in with him and see how things have changed and what advice he has for new fathers.

Meeting with Dr. Keyes for the first time as an adult was also, perhaps, the only time that I was permitted to keep my pants on for our entire chat. He looked about the same. He still exudes a comforting, deliberate, soft-spoken authority. Though he commented that I looked different—"I think I used to be taller than you"—he was kind enough not to mention my weight (I wore the large vest).

We went around the corner for lunch and, trying to be healthy, I ordered the chicken Caesar. He showed me up with half a veggie sandwich, a bowl of tomato bisque, and a cup of hot chocolate. He never got the bisque, and it occurred to me that, perhaps, that's the real secret to keeping as fit as a doc: letting some food go. The men of my family haven't been without a side dish in two generations.

When I conduct interviews over a meal, I usually try to keep my questions sparse and make sure my subject has a chance to eat his food. But with only half a sandwich and a missing cup of soup to tangle with, I jumped right in.

What, I asked, was the biggest change in parents that he'd seen in the last thirty years? How had parents evolved in the years between my birth and the birth of my kids?

"Parents," he said, "have become remarkably more protective of their kids than they were when I started."

This is not surprising. There's a bumper crop of books and essays decrying paranoid, helicopter parents who won't leave their kids alone on the playground or in the classroom. But Dr. Keyes says the problem starts much sooner than the day kids are old enough to walk out of their sight. It starts before they're born.

Expectant parents today pour over books and the Internet looking for ways to protect and prepare for their unborn children. After the birth, things get into high gear. They keep their children as far away from peanuts, Pepsi, and Enfamil as possible, thinking not just about a child's health, but his future. There's the SAT to think about, college, and the best school for three-year-olds. By the time these protected bodies reach school age, they're regimented into the ground, with every move and hour of their day optimized to protect them from mediocrity and land-grant institutions.

The problem with constantly optimizing for the next level, Keyes says, is that nothing is ever good enough.

"You know, even if you get into Harvard, then you gotta make good grades in Harvard. And once you get out of Harvard you've got to land a job at the best law firm in the country. Nothing is ever good enough, and once you get there you realize that even though you've achieved that you've still gotta look at greater things. What still do you need to achieve?"

The secret to happy, healthy kids, he said, isn't an abundance of caution, but an abundance of love.

"I usually tell younger parents that you can't hold your child too much. The more you carry them around, the less fussy they'll be. Eventually, you'll have to get to a point where you have to say no sometimes, and that's OK. Just decide the boundaries. Decide what you can handle, what the right boundaries are for your particular house and for your household. I think it's really that if the child feels loved and accepted and listened to, then everything else will fall into place."

The problem, he says, is that these days most kids don't feel accepted and listened to. He went on to tell me that years ago, he saw a study that showed that kids need at least fifteen minutes of undivided attention every day. It doesn't sound like much, but, thinking about myself, I know that even though I'm around my kids for large chunks of the day, I don't give either of them fifteen minutes of undivided attention every day. Neither did Dr. Keyes.

"If I did it again, that's what I'd try to do," he said. "I'd try to sit down with them for fifteen minutes and just listen to what they had to say. Some kids are a little more verbal than others. But kids just need our time and they need us to listen to them."

As we were wrapping up lunch, I bounced a theory off Dr. Keyes that I'd carried around since the months before Thomas was born. Though I have nothing against prepregnancy classes (well, not much), I came away from the one I took with Betsy thinking that the really important stuff we needed to know before we brought our baby home from the hospital could be put on a 3x5 notecard.

"Absolutely," he said. "That's exactly right."

My card would include swaddling, soothing, feeding, and cleaning. When I asked Dr. Keyes for his, he was much more holistic.

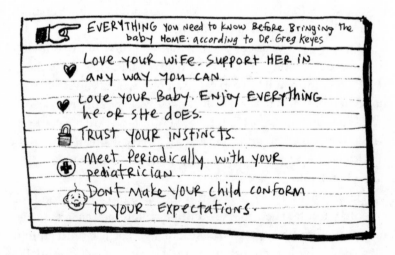

EVERYTHING You Need to Know Before Bringing the baby HOME: according to Dr. Greg keyes

- ♥ Love youR wife. SuppoRt HER iN any way you can.
- ♥ Love youR Baby. ENJoy EVERything he oR sHe doEs.
- 🔒 TRust youR iNstiNcts.
- ➕ Meet periodically with youR pediatRician.
- 👶 DoNt make youR child conform to youR Expectations.

"It would be love your wife and support her in any way you can; love your baby, and enjoy everything he or she does; trust your instincts; meet periodically with your pediatrician; and don't make your child conform to your expectations.

"I don't know if I have any other wisdom, but there are a lot of other things that I look at myself and say 'did I do that for my kids growing up?' You know, we just try to do the best we can. And life's tough. You've got a lot of demands. But, it's a matter of keeping your priorities straight. And if your wife and family are high on your priority list, then that will show up in your kids and they'll really feel loved and nurtured and feel like they've got the confidence to approach life."

Thanks, Doc.

But, of Course, Take the Birthing Course

Your baby is about sixteen inches long from head to toe.

Your lady has enrolled both of you in the six-week childbirth course.

The situation: You think you can get out of the classes because you've got a 3x5 card.

The reality: The classes are a good chance to familiarize yourself with many of the situations that could arise before, during, and after the birth. But, more importantly, she'll feel better if you take the birthing course. And making her feel better is one of your primary jobs.

Just because the most important things you need to know before you bring your baby home can be put on a 3x5 card doesn't get us out of the six-week class—or whatever class(es) your lady wants to take. That it's not essential to raising a child doesn't mean it's not important.

"First of all, the reason that you attend prenatal classes is not for the baby, it's not for you, it's for your wife, because she needs to know that you support her," Dr. Keyes told me. "And the most important relationship you have is husband and wife, not father to child, not mother to child, but husband to wife. Because you are the family—you and your wife are the family—the kids are linked to you for a period of time and then they go on their way and they establish their own. But you've gotta be able to be in those classes so your wife knows that you care enough about what she's going through."

Dr. Stella Dantas, an obstetrician and Portland Trailblazers fan I spoke to in Oregon, told me that this thinking crosses over into prenatal check-ups as well. She doesn't think men have to accompany their women to every appointment, but the more they can be at the more they can empathize with her and stay in the loop with what's going on with her body—and the baby's.

"I think it helps both parties," she says. "I think it helps the woman because if she didn't quite understand something or wants to talk about it again after the appointment, she has somebody to bounce it off of. But also, it helps keep men feel involved in the pregnancy, because they don't get to experience any of the physical changes. This is a way for them to be engaged."

This next suggestion is going to send you into stitches, but I'm gonna say it anyway: the classes and doctor's appointments can become like dates. When you're finished laughing at that last one, hear me out.

Right now, you're used to being with each other, and just each other, any time that you'd like. But when you have a child, you have to plan on times to be together, just the two of you. And your definition of "together" time will start to evolve.

When Betsy was pregnant with Lucy, she planned her OB appointments for the mornings, when Thomas was at preschool. We'd go together, and sometimes go out to lunch afterward. These are some of the few times we'd been out to lunch together, just the two of us, in four years. We were both working and raising a child. If we were alone together, it was usually at night or on a rare weekend away. Lunch on a school day was a pleasant rarity.

Dr. Dantas says to take advantage of all the opportunities for togetherness before the baby's born. She says that a lot of times couples get so caught up in preparing for the arrival of their child—the shopping, the reading, the stressing—that they forget to invest in each other.

"Make time to spend with each other before that newborn period, and to take the time to nourish your relationship," she says. "Go see a movie, go to dinner, go see a show, go and do all those things that in that acute postpartum period you're not going to be able to do."

Week 31

Just Do Everything Yourself

Your baby is hiccupping.

Your lady is a bit more forgetful than usual. This is called pregnancy brain.

The situation: You're taking the pregnancy classes but hardly retain any of the tips.

The reality: It's not pregnancy brain. Nobody remembers anything. Just remember one thing: do everything yourself.

to do:
☐ learn how to change a diaper
☐ put crib together
☐

As much as I like to grouse about the instructor who taught our six-week course—the one who thinks women should spend the first year of their babies' lives barefoot and breast-feeding at home—I have to admit that one of the best pieces of parenting advice I've ever heard came out of her mouth during the class. Well, technically, after the class.

We'd kinda paired off with another couple during sessions, and when the last class was calling it quits, the male half of our friends and I were making our way to the door, when he took a turn toward the instructor. He said thanks for everything and asked one final question. I wish I had written down his exact words because they startled me so much, but it was something to the effect of: so, what should we do?

Seriously. We'd just spent six, ass-busting weeks in plastic chairs putting diapers on dolls and going over every conceivable problem that could arise during the birth, and he wanted to know, you know, what should we do? It wouldn't have surprised me if the instructor had shot back: "Um, yeah, that's actually what we have been talking about for the last month and a half and I'm glad to see it sunk in." But she didn't.

Instead, she gave us the most useful piece of information she'd uttered yet: just do everything yourself. After the baby's born, you be the one to change the diapers. You watch the way the staff gives the baby a bath. You watch how they deal with the umbilical cord. You swaddle the baby. And do it all in the hospital so your lady can get some rest and you are under the watchful eye of paid professionals who turn out babies all day, every day. The nurses and doctors will provide all the help that you need. And it's not just that they're helpful and generous, it's that they would really rather not do it themselves.

I took her advice to heart. I was the one who changed most of the diapers for the first forty-eight hours (inevitably, the streak had to come to an end). I accompanied Thomas to the weird room where the nurse sponged him down for the first time. I got a lesson in bottle feeding from the nurse on duty. When Lucy was born, I was kind of concerned with the difference between how to clean up and change a girl than a boy. The nurses were very helpful: just wipe from the top down. Don't wipe up. Don't let something from the bottom get into the top.

Getting a handle on the basics from the start is advantageous in several ways. Of course, it helps your lady get some rest (and security), but it also sets a good precedent. If you can do everything (feeding is kind of a murky ground here) that she can, then it removes barriers for spending time with the baby and gives all of you freedom and flexibility. If only one of you knows how to take care of the baby, then that person always has to be there to take care of the baby.

Plus, a sense of freedom and accomplishment comes in being able to take a newborn out on your own, and in knowing how to deal with anything that comes your way.

week 32

Make Time for the Two of You

Your baby sleeps more than 90 percent of the day (enjoy it while you can).

Your lady's belly has been interfering with her sleep.

The situation: You're getting ready to become a power trio.

The reality: It's a good time to plan a postbaby, no baby, mini vacation.

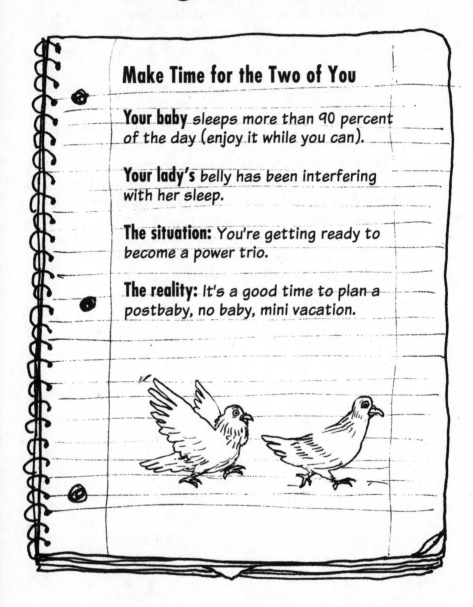

*T*hrough the years, Betsy and I have made a habit of staying at the Waterstreet Hotel in Port Townsend. It's really not fancy. There are no telephones in the rooms. Many of them, in fact, don't have toilets. But if you're feeling flush, you can get your own can. On our last trip, I treated my hardworking woman to a room— with a shower and everything.

Port Townsend's a tourist town that specializes in shops geared toward women over sixty. But the place has charm and a salty underbelly. At the turn of the century, it was a hub of West Coast shanghaiing. And to this day, the locals—a bit more disheveled than you'd expect in a city of doilies and used books— have a suspicious, plotting way about them.

Sitting on the deck of the restaurant the first night, it was clear that we were all there for the same reason. The deck was filled with couples, and the adjoining roof littered with pigeons. While the rest of us were getting in a meal and a couple of drinks before we retired to our rooms for the evening's activities, the pigeons were putting up no pretenses. The roof of the building below us was lousy with uncontrollable pigeon sex.

Every time I looked over, I saw the same pigeon waddle his way to a different, unsuspecting bird, ruffle his feathers, and mount up. He didn't stop. Some of the other couples started figuring out what was going on and got all kinds of embarrassed in their Chardonnay. I'd never seen pigeons having sex before, but it makes sense that they'd be doing it in Port Townsend. Everyone needs a weekend away. Even pigeons.

This was one of those weekends away when the only agenda was to get away. I know a lot of couples who get ambitious on their days off: they go hiking, camping, or better themselves by the history found in museums. We seek out cable television, a room with blinds, and take-out pizza.

Having kids is exhausting physically, of course. But it's mentally taxing as well. I suppose I should be worried to death about how my son is doing when he's not in our company, but I sleep like a baby when the well-being of my child is temporarily out of my hands. This trip to Port Townsend was a mental vacation as much as a physical one. Which is why we opted for Tom Cruise flicks with commercials rather than a walk through one of the area's many historical sites.

Betsy and I didn't go on a *babymoon*—that "one last hoorah" before the baby is born. And, frankly, I've always been kind of opposed to the idea. Not that I don't see the appeal. A few months before Thomas was born, we visited Tyler and pregnant Chelsea in wine country, and it was wonderful to have two designated drivers to drive around their designated assholes. But it wasn't a babymoon. It was a visit to see friends.

If there's a trip or experience you've been meaning to have that's going to be tough when you have kids, go for it. Get as much time together as you can. If you feel like going on a big vacation before the due date, well, there's never anything wrong with getting some R&R, especially if one of you has someone in utero.

My first problem with the babymoon idea is that it's kind of too late. It makes about as much sense as a Hollywood bachelor party. If you're going to have one last night out with the boys to get wasted and wake up with chicks you've just met, it kind of makes more sense to do that *before* you fall in love with the person you want to spend the rest of the world with. By the same token, if you're going to go on a splendid vacation to Europe or Cancun or, um, wine country, doesn't it make a little more sense to do it before your lady is pregnant, when she can lose herself in the local brews and the sight of herself in a bikini?

But my principal problem with the babymoon concept is that it's a "last hoorah" before the baby comes, and that what comes next isn't a hoorah. And I think it can become a self-fulfilling prophesy.

I recently caught up with an acquaintance for the first time since he went on his babymoon—replete with Facebook pictures with smiles and microbrews in the pool (no, she wasn't drinking)—and had a baby. It had been almost two years since the birth, and we were both at the opening of a documentary. This, he explained, was one of his only nights out since the baby had been born. In fact, he and his wife rarely took the baby out of the house. She stayed home. He went to work, came home, and hung out with the kid. They were both too tired to do anything else. It doesn't have to be that way. Having a baby doesn't have to mean the end of fun, and it shouldn't be the end of one-on-one time between you and your lady.

Whether you're going to treat your pregnant wife to a few days at the beach and spa (and if you can afford it, do it) and call it a babymoon or not, I'd like to suggest penciling in an additional item on the schedule: a weekend away for just the two of you sometime after the birth. I'm not suggesting this because it's something we did. I'm making the suggestion because I wish we had. We got away for the first time when Thomas was about four months old, somewhat last minute. It's the kind of thing I wish, from the moment he was born, that we'd had on the schedule.

I've bent over backward trying to make the case that having a baby is an amazing, life-altering event that has been a positive change to me and every one of the men I spoke to while writing this book. But I'm not Pollyannaish about the weeks and months after birth. They're hard. Sure, they're incredibly joyous, but, like most things in life that are worth anything, they're also a lot of work. There are sleepless nights. Personal fuses get burned down to nothing. Tempers flare. Things are said. You'll love your baby in a way that you didn't think possible. You'll also reach a level of fatigue—and possibly despair—that you've never been to.

This is why it would be nice to have something for the two of you to look forward to doing together, to remind each other how you got into this beautiful mess in the first place. It will feel good during those endless nights to remember that there is a weekend in the future during which you can recharge your batteries and be alone with the person you make babies with.

In doing hundreds of interviews and surveys with married couples, Dr. Coltrane, the sociologist at the University of Oregon, told me that one of the best pieces of advice he gleaned from the results was for couples to make time for each other.

"I heard over and over again that those people who could maintain that part of their relationship and have date nights and have some time away from kids so that they could be partners together fared better in terms of their marital satisfaction."

It might feel selfish to think about getting away without the baby. But keeping things strong between the two of you— whether through weekends away or nights out alone—is good for the baby.

"If you neglect the spousal relationship, you're really neglecting the baby, because who's the major role models for that baby? It's the two parents," says Dr. Libby, the sex therapist. "If they're not affectionate with each other, that affects their emotional and sexual development. That's not a good thing. And I think a lot of people don't think of those things."

In other words: don't let the pigeons have all the fun.

Week 33

Forget the Garden, Get a Crock-Pot

Your baby weighs about four and a half pounds.

Your lady has put on about five times that.

The situation: You're doing most of the cooking while your lady puts her swollen feet up.

The reality: Set reasonable expectations for yourself. Get a Crock-Pot.

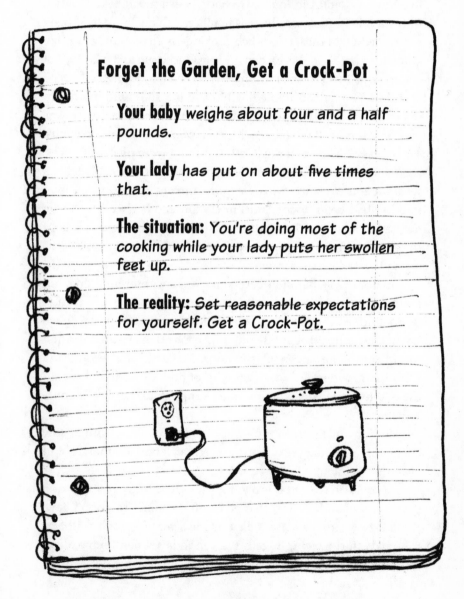

The summer that I met Betsy in Wisconsin, I made a pit stop at my uncle Ben's house on the drive back to school. Since he lived in Iowa and I in Idaho, we hadn't seen much of each other. But as a college professor, he was familiar with my lifestyle. When I mentioned that I didn't do much cooking on account of being lazy and fairly useless in the kitchen, he introduced me to the Crock-Pot and a recipe that I'm about to share with you (see below).

I drove home and immediately gave it a shot with my roommate, Bill. Everything Ben told me about the miracle device was true. It was easy. It was cheap. More importantly, it was delicious. There wasn't a scrap of meat left. But there were plenty of juices, a bone, and some fat that sat covered in our slow cooker for a week before we started the cleanup conversation. A week later nothing had been done. And I'm certain another week went by before I removed the lid, walked out to the Dumpster, and caught myself gagging as the top layer of hardened fat shifted to release a smell that I'll never forget.

I'm not sure what kind of a coin toss I lost on round one, but after our second Crock of melted, fall-off-the-bone pork, Bill and I decided to select a party responsible for cleanup the only way we knew how: with an eggnog-chugging contest. Bill poured the first round into large, green plastic cups. We tied. The second and third rounds went the same way. Out of nog, we each took a handle of the Crock, walked out to the Dumpster, and did the honors together.

What my uncle hadn't told me was that cooking with a slow cooker is a lot like sex: during is great, after is ethereal, but cleanup is a bitch.

You don't have to be broke to know that $1.69 is a hell of a price for a pound of meat that melts off the bone. You don't have to be lazy to appreciate a delicious meal that takes no skill and minimal effort to whip together. Even today, when I have a few more nickels in my pocket and enough muscle memory in my fingers to produce a passable meal on short order, I still find my-self drawn to the slow cooker. There are some things that can only be made better with time, heat, and a lot of fat.

Like great pieces of music and art, everyone finds the Crock-Pot at a different point in their lives. I found it in college when I was at my laziest. Andrew Smiler discovered it after his wife gave birth to their first child, when he was at his most exhausted. That's the beauty of a tool that's as brilliantly engineered as the Crock-Pot: it's as useful for the laziest members of our society as it is the hardest working.

"One of the challenges for new parents is in some ways learn-ing about stamina, learning how much energy you have, and how much it takes to get through the week," says Smiler, who, in addition to being a Crock-Pot aficionado, is a family therapist and psychologist who studies masculinity. "And once you know that: what can you reasonably accomplish in a week?"

This is where the Crock-Pot came into the Smiler family's life. With he and his wife both working, Smiler realized they weren't going to have the energy to produce a quality meal on the fly ev-ery night. They preferred to spend the hours after work fawning over their new baby. So they planned out their meals a week in advance and did as much food prep as possible on the weekends. This prep included chopping up vegetables and protein and put-ting them in a large piece of Tupperware marked with something like "Tuesday/Crock-Pot." Tuesday morning, all they had to do was dump the ingredients into the Crock Pot and come home to a fully-cooked meal.

"For us, that was part of managing our energy and our re-sources and our time," he says. "One of us can do food prep while one of us is with the infant. And there were times when we would actually have a babysitter over and the two of us would be in the kitchen for an hour and a half preparing the next week's food."

I've never planned that far ahead. But I think it's genius.

* * *

It goes without saying that sharpening your Crock-Pot skills will come in handy when your child starts to eat solid foods. It's the perfect way for overworked parents to feed their families healthy meals. Don't let Michelle Obama—or anyone else—tell you that a rooftop garden needs to be involved.

A few years after I settled into my Crock-Pot lifestyle, a time when Barack Obama was bringing change to the nation and Instagram didn't exist, the first lady of the United States of America decided to tackle the country's childhood obesity epidemic.

"Back when many of us were growing up, we led lives that kept most of us at a pretty healthy weight," she wrote in *Newsweek*. "We walked to school every day . . . and ate home-cooked meals that always seemed to have a vegetable on the plate."

To solve the problem, Mrs. Obama posed for pictures in the White House vegetable garden and championed local farmers' markets. The solution to childhood obesity, according to the first lady, was for parents to start growing their own tomatoes.

She was hardly the only one. You can't walk down the street without seeing a twenty-something green thumb wearing an "eat local" T-shirt; and you can't open your Facebook feed without someone (or some headline) telling you you're not feeding your family well enough (or as good as they are).

Mrs. Obama's nostalgia, in particular, was curious. Back in the halcyon days of healthy waistlines that she espoused, most mothers stayed at home to raise children and cook meals. But America is (thankfully) a different place today. The kind of place where same-sex couples can marry, you can legally buy marijuana, and a majority of voters raised their hands for a black candidate for president. Twice.

In 2012, the year Michelle Obama released her book, *American Grown: The Story of the White House Kitchen Garden and Gardens Across America*, both parents were working outside the home in more than 59 percent of households, according to the Bureau of Labor Statistics. In 1975, when Mrs. Obama was ten years old, less than half of mothers worked outside the home. By 2015, more than two-thirds did.

Parents don't have the time to fuss over home-cooked meals and a vegetable garden the way they once did (if they ever did). Making parents feel like they've underperformed by not shucking homegrown corn after a long day at work and a two-hour commute isn't going to make any family healthier.

It's not that Mrs. Obama was wrong to tell parents they were setting their kids up for early-onset diabetes. She's wrong about the solution: it's not rooftop gardens and farmers' markets. It's the Crock-Pot.

What's important is for kids to get a well-rounded meal, to eat some vegetables, to spend a little less time at Burger King. The Crock-Pot is as simple as it gets. It's easier than a microwave: you put your ingredients inside, turn it on, and forget about it for eight to ten hours.

So, give yourself a break. Don't feel like your kids or your pregnant wife will be malnourished if you don't pull their veggies from the garden behind your chicken coop. The onions you find at Target will do just fine.

My Uncle Ben's Slow Cooker Recipe

CRock®

4-8 Pounds of Pork Shoulder

1 Packet of French Onion Soup Mix

12 ounces of Coke Zero * (Feel free to substitute dark seasonal Beer)

1 Bag of Mini carrots   1 Brown Potato Chopped   2 celery stalks Chopped

**(I really have an uncle Ben.
This recipe does not call for rice.)**

Add all of the ingredients to a slow cooker before you leave for work in the morning. Be sure to leave as much fat as possible on the pork, and leave the fat side up. Set the temperature to low. It'll be done when you get home, as long as that's between eight and twelve hours later. Yes, you can brown the meat first if you like. No, it's not mandatory.

---

* Uncle Ben actually suggested full-octane Coke, but I find it works just as good with Coke Zero.

While I've got you in the kitchen . . .
poach your lady an egg (Bill Nye style)

Eggs carry many benefits for pregnant women. Among them, according to a 2012 Cornell University study, is choline, which can reduce a baby's future response to stress, and help ward off hypertension and diabetes. One a day will do the trick. If you want to impress your lady, poach that egg.

I know, I know, I just finished lambasting Michelle Obama for making parents feel like failures for not tilling their own soil, and now I'm suggesting you attempt to jump the Grand Canyon of egg cooking on two hours of sleep. But it's not like that at all. At least that's what Bill Nye once told me.

When I asked the Science Guy what he likes to do in his free time, he told me that he likes to poach eggs. He thinks you should, too. "People are spooked by poaching an egg. People: boil water, swirl it, put a little vinegar in, swirl it, put the egg in. Three minutes. Take the egg out. Enjoy it."

If your lady can't stand eggs, don't sweat it: you can find that choline in broccoli.

week 34

Free Time Isn't a Luxury.
It's a Necessity

Your baby is the size of a honeydew.

Your lady is working and cooking a baby.

The situation: You're talking about the work/chore schedule for after the birth.

The reality: Leave some time for yourself. It's good for all of you.

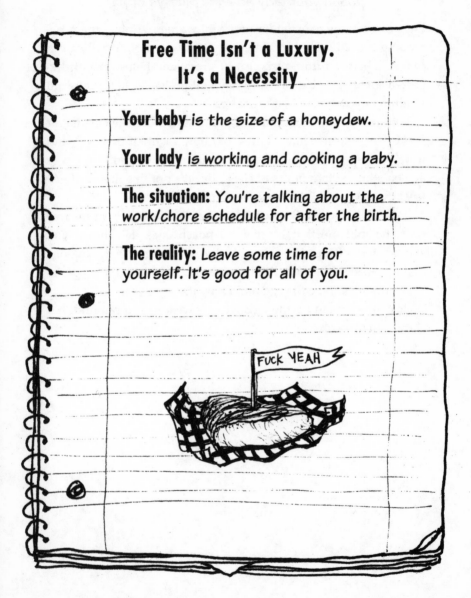

I'm sitting upstairs at a coffee shop in Seattle feeling guilty. I woke up when Thomas got into my side of the bed at 6:30. I got out of bed twenty minutes later, when I could no longer in good conscience tell Thomas "in just a minute" when he asked "can we get up now?"

Lucy woke up a few minutes later. I made the bottle. Betsy fed her. Thomas played and danced around while I boiled eggs, made a PB&J, and packed his lunch.

I left the house at 7:50 and started my thirty-minute walk to the ferry. By 7:57, a stranger on the street and I corralled a lost dog. I was on my usual route and knew exactly where the mutt lived. It was a small dog, but unfortunately had spent the morning rolling around in urine. I was in my sixteen-year-old red cap, black T-shirt, and Converse knock-offs. She was wearing a nice work outfit, so I offered to carry the beast to the front door. After five minutes of knocking, a weary old lady in a nightgown came to the door. No, she was not the owner of the dog. It belonged in the purple house across the street. Mission accomplished.

By this time I'd missed my 8 a.m. call with the editor of this book. But, a working dad like myself, he was pulling a shift from home and didn't seem to mind that I called him a bit late.

I worked on the ferry, then read a book about the topic of my next book on the bus as I made my way to a meeting with Aaron, the illustrator of this book. He was inside juggling sketches and Baxter, who spent the morning listening to The Clash's *London Calling*.

After Aaron met with me to go over illustrations, Baxter was going to take a nap, then the two of them were going to work a shift at the bookstore. Aaron explained that if he tried to get Baxter to sleep in the Ergo while he was pricing tomes, he couldn't get the boy to sleep. But if he just said "fuck it" and left him to his own devices, he'd drift off in no time. When he's done with work, he'll head home, make dinner, then do the dishes while Jessixa puts the pup in his pajamas. Once Baxter's asleep, Aaron will pour a couple of gin and tonics, and they'll sketch away at their respective projects until they pass out on the couch.

After our meeting, I started walking to the bus, but noticed a plastic lawn chair and a rickety table in a patch of shade on the lawn in front of Aaron's building. I sat down and quickly pulled out my laptop and called Jill Ellis, the coach of the US women's national soccer team. I was collecting a tech recommendation for a piece in the *Wall Street Journal*, and she suggested the Life360 app, which lets her family members keep in touch by seeing exactly where they are at every moment. Sometimes Jill can be on the road for three out of four weeks a month—and was in the middle of a nationwide World Cup victory tour that would dovetail into preparations for the Olympics when we spoke. Life360 lets her daughter know where she is at all times—including whether she's in the air or on the ground available for a call.

After our chat, I made my way to the bus stop. I was starving and started daydreaming about barbecued pork in the International District. At just that moment, I realized that Betsy had tucked some brisket into my lunch bag before I left. I gave my world and my wife a little "fuck yeah" and dove into the salted, smoky beef.

Just then, a beat-up van driven by a dude in a crooked-billed cap pulled up in front of me. He ignored me, flipped a u-ey, and parked across the street. A minute later, a happy bro walked up to the van's window, paid for his weed, and handed the driver a Popsicle. He wasn't just picking up his order, he was pimping his Popsicle company.

On the bus, full of brisket and wearing a smug grin, I texted Betsy to thank her for the snacks and asked her how her day was going.

It'd been a busy one. She'd already piled Thomas and Lucy into the car, dropped Thomas off at school, and went to the first session of MOPS (Mothers of Preschoolers) for the year and was waiting outside preschool for the T-Man to get out. She was still recovering from the day before, when she made appointments for her interior design business between running errands, feeding and changing Lucy, getting Thomas to and from school, writing a blog post for the local paper, and, oh, yeah, putting a coat of paint on the three chairs she's been working on. When I reached her, she said she was doing alright, but, oh, yeah, she forgot to put that other blog post up this morning.

Tomorrow, Saturday, Betsy's got a half-day meeting with a ladies group, and I'm taking Thomas and Lucy to breakfast at the new Sonic with my dad. I have a gluten intolerance and can't deal with dairy very well, but I'm going to eat the hell out of some burgers, fries, and milkshake (for the one and only time). Then I'm going to take the kids to the local sporting goods store to get Thomas some new shoes for his first season of soccer (it's indoor, so cleats won't work).

Once Betsy's done with her meeting in the afternoon, we'll all go home, play with the kids, make dinner, put them to bed, then get to work on our respective projects before watching part of a movie and falling asleep. Sunday morning, we'll make breakfast early and juggle the kids for a few minutes before I tear down our rotting fence, mow the lawn, and generally winterize our yard.

But it's still Friday afternoon. It's 2:11 at the coffee shop. I know what I'm doing tomorrow and I know what Betsy's been doing today. I've been meaning to go buy a new hat, because I bought the one I'm wearing now in the summer of 1999, and it smells like the underside of a public toilet (or maybe that's the residual smell of the piss-stained dog I found this morning). The Mariners's team store is a half mile down the street. If I leave now, I can spend an hour strolling in the sun and picking out a new hat that I'll wear—if the life expectancy of my current one is any guide—until I'm fifty. But I don't think I'm gonna. I feel guilty. It'd be too much fun. Betsy doesn't get a break this afternoon, or this weekend.

Neither does Aaron or Jessixa. Or the coach of the US women's national soccer team. Or the weed-smoking Popsicle entrepreneur who can't stop hustling for a minute while he picks up an eighth at the curb. The hustle doesn't stop for any of us. But it should.

Free time isn't an extravagance. It's essential. And it should be put on the schedule, even when you can't find room. It's something that I feel guilty about. There's always something else that needs doing. But we all need to take care of ourselves.

"One of the big differences that we see for couples once they become parents—and this is well established in thirty or forty years of research—is a drop in their free time and the activities, call them hobbies if you want or time with friends, than they used to have," says Smiler, the couples therapist. "One of the correlates of that is that if you're not doing fun stuff with your time because now you're putting all of your time and energy into your kid, then there's just a lot less happiness and a lot more stress in your life and you've lost these ways to deal with it."

This isn't just something we should shrug off as the nature of parenting. It's bad for the kid, too.

"We know that kids under a year—and certainly kids over a year—do respond negatively to parents who are highly stressed," Smiler says. "And one of the things we know in general is that people who are highly stressed tend to be kind of short-tempered and grumpy. So, if you're really stressed out and your infant needs something, maybe you're a little bit less patient with the child."

I've done a lousy job putting free time on the calendar, and a worse time making it possible for Betsy—who fields the majority of the kid-time—to feel good about having time to kick back and do whatever she likes.

Smiler suggests that couples who can afford it designate a night each week for yourselves (you've got Tuesday nights, I've got Wednesday nights, etc.). If both of you have that time, then there's no reason to feel guilty that the other person is left holding the bag.

I like the idea—it feels kind of like what I hear from people who are responsible with money and say things like, "You should feel good about spending your disposable income." I think a night each week for both of us is a bit much (at least to start), but a night or two a month is doable, and would probably make the whole family feel better.

Having some kind of regular time to unwind is the kind of thing you can plan for in the months leading up to the birth, which could blunt at least a little bit of the preventable stress.

"I think it's very important for everyone's mental health," Smiler says. "Having that free time and time that you can use to relax helps the individual and then that certainly feeds into how they're interacting with the partner and the kid. For some families that's really not an option—if you have two adults who have three jobs. But if at all possible, it is a very good thing to have."

See, you heard it from a doctor: time for yourself isn't just about you. Maybe it will be easier to justify if you remind yourself when you're at the bar on Monday night that you're doing it for the baby.

With that in mind, I'm gonna go buy myself a new hat.

Week 35

There Will Be a Parent Running Point (The Other One Is Helping)

Your baby has put his head down for evacuation.

Your lady's feet no longer fit into her tennis shoes.

The situation: Your lady has gone on maternity leave, and plans to go back in a few months.

The reality: There's a good chance she's not going back to work.

Last night I killed the kitchen with Clorox while listening to Tom Waits, got excited, and went through a bit too much gin. Getting out of bed was a bit harder than usual.

I did manage to get up when Thomas asked me if I'd play with him. We messed around with Duplo blocks (they're the big version of Legos) until we heard Lucy stirring. We got her out of the crib, and I made her a bottle of formula just as Betsy emerged from the bedroom. She took Lucy and the bottle and I hit the kitchen to make breakfast. By the time Betsy and Thomas were on the way out the door, Thomas was wearing his new, blue kicks and Betsy was looking all kinds of lovely in her new top (or whatever they're calling it). Even Lucy had changed duds once already. I was still in yesterday's black V-neck and the Eddie Bauer pajama pants my mom got me for Christmas what had to have been a decade ago.

I put Lucy down for a nap after they left, and spent a half hour at work in the living room before Lucy woke up for some peas and rice cereal. She's been eating like a champ lately, real food (if we're considering baby-food peas real food, and compared to formula, we are), and, as a consequence, has been dropping some solids. When I changed a load after her second breakfast, I got a little excited at the thought of Lucy growing up, and a little sad at the thought of her growing up.

Once I cleaned her up, I finally got out of my pajamas, tossed on a fresh V-neck and my new Mariners's hat, and we hit my old walking route—into downtown, through the park, and across the community college campus, all in all about four miles.

After we got home, I gave Lucy a bath, laid her on the living room carpet in a black onesie, and was mildly horrified to see how much debris her shirt picked up in a matter of seconds. So, I put Lucy in her bouncer and gave the house a quick vacuum—making sure to not put the vacuum away so that there would be no mistaking my achievement. Betsy's meeting went longer than she expected, and when she got home, she was impressed to see all that I'd accomplished. She gave me a kiss and thanked me for "helping out so much."

I used to hate it when she said things like that. It made me feel like a babysitter who popped over to lend a hand. I didn't think I was "helping" her with the kids and the house. I felt like I was just doing my share, as she was. Of course, she didn't mean anything by it. She wasn't suggesting that I was the junior partner in the raising of the kids. Regardless, she was right: I am the junior partner in this. I am helping out.

Yes, I can change Lucy's diaper and put her into a fresh onesie, no problem. But I don't know what size clothes she's wearing. I just open up her drawer, pull something out, and put it on her. Yes, I can feed her the smashed up peas and the rice cereal that says "oatmeal" on the box, but I didn't pick it out at the store; I didn't know it was time for her to move on to "solids." Yes, I'm happy to go to the store when Thomas picks out his new shoes—but I didn't realize he needed a new pair. Yes, I'm happy to read Thomas a book, but it wasn't my idea to make reading an integral part of his daily routine. Yes, I can give Lucy a bath. But I didn't find the inflatable yellow duck that's the perfect pool size for a toddler and makes bath time a breeze.

In some ways, that's the nature of our arrangement: I'm the primary breadwinner and Betsy helps out, bringing in some money. We can't do it without either. She's the primary caregiver, and I help out. We can't do it without either.

But even if you and your lady both work full-time and you strive to equally share the child-rearing duties, she's probably the one that's keeping the family engine running, while you shovel in coal.

In a humbling piece in the *New York Times* entitled "Mom: The Designated Worrier," Judith Shulevitz explained that these behind-the-scene tasks are called "worry work," and that they're predominantly handled by women—even in relationships that espouse a 50–50 split. "Sociological studies of heterosexual couples from all strata of society," she wrote, "confirm that, by and large, mothers draft the to-do lists while fathers pick and choose among the items."

Busted.

What's more, men are often congratulated for their efforts, while a woman's Herculean parenting feats are ignored. One friend put it to me this way: when her husband takes the kids to the grocery store, the little old ladies throw him a parade. When she does the same, they take down the streamers. I've seen this myself, plenty of times.

When Thomas was stroller sized and my friend Brian had a daughter in the same demographic, we took the kids for a stroll by the water. When we were pushing our kids along, an older gentleman smiled at us and inquired good-naturedly: "Giving the ladies the afternoon off, huh?!?!"

More recently, when I took Thomas and Lucy to the high school to kick it on the track, Thomas hit a wall and asked to ride home on my shoulders. So, we made the four-block trek home with me pushing Lucy in the stroller and Thomas half falling asleep on my head. An older dude with a wide grin saw us, gave me a thumbs-up and said: "Super dad! Go dad!"

When people see a dad schlepping two tired kids home, he's a hero. When a mom does it, people wonder why she's let them skip a nap.

There's nothing we can do about the general public, but we can recognize the unrecognized, and not pretend that we're super dads because we know where to find the vacuum.

Or, better yet, we can take on a bit of the worry work ourselves.

Week 36

To Paternity Leave (and Beyond!)

Your baby is in her sixth pound.

Your lady may have leaky breasts (that's colostrum, not breast milk, but it's close).

The situation: You're making final paternity leave negotiations with your employer.

The reality: It's not only about you: paternity leave can be good for everyone.

When Jeff Hill and his wife were expecting their seventh child, Jeff approached his boss at IBM and said that when the baby was born, he wanted to take a year off. It took him an hour to convince his manager that he wasn't playing a practical joke. He didn't understand why Hill would want to take the time off or how he would support himself. But at the end of the meeting, he told Hill he'd look into it.

Two weeks later, he came back with some good news: the company would give Hill two weeks off with pay, but that he was too valuable to the company to lose for an entire year. "Well, that's really the wrong answer," Hill responded. "Could you ask somebody else?"

Hill's fifth and sixth children were twins. And shortly after the birth, one of them passed away. His wife, Juanita, became pregnant again, by accident, soon after. She wasn't feeling well. She had five living children to care for and had just said good-bye to her sixth. He had just spent several years in the IBM human resources department. At the end of his tenure, he had observed the company adopt several gender-neutral policies. Technically, men and women were both eligible for a year of unpaid leave after the birth of a child, with their jobs guaranteed when they got back. It's just that men weren't asking for it.

Another two weeks passed and Hill's manager told him that he had more good news. He remembers the exchange going like this:

> **Manager:** The company will give you two weeks of paid leave and allow you to take six weeks of deferred vacation. So, that will give you two months at home. And after two months at home, for sure, you'll want to be coming back to work.
> **Hill:** Well, tell me, what's the difference between me and Suzy? She had just as good a performance evaluation as me and she

got a year off. And how about Beverly? She had just the same evaluation as me. Why did she get a year off? What's the difference between me and them?

Manager: Don't you know what the difference is between you and them?

Hill: Well, yes. I just want to hear it from my IBM manager that the reason I'm not getting this leave is because I'm a man.

Manager: I think I'll check with somebody else.

Eventually, Hill's manager offered him terms he could accept: two weeks off with pay, six weeks of deferred vacation, and then he had to come back to work for a day. If, after that one day back at work, Hill wanted to go back on leave, he could take up to a year of unpaid leave, and the company would welcome him back any time.

"And, so, that's what I did," Hill says. "And it changed my life."

By the time his seventh child was born, Hill had been at IBM for a dozen years, and had never been at the house when his kids got home from school. He had never seen what the day-to-day life was like inside his home.

"I learned that I really liked it. I really liked being involved in my children's lives and being there when they came home from school, and taking care of them. We were very, very frugal. We didn't spend any money. We didn't ever go out to eat. We ate bulk food. We did everything we could do to conserve resources."

He went back to work after about eight months away "a changed man." He was no longer anxious to spend twelve hours a day away from home. And he began to seek out new opportunities.

An executive named Barbara Wood offered him a huge promotion at IBM headquarters in Westchester County, New York. Hill was interested in the job, but didn't think it would be financially responsible to raise a large family in such an expensive zip code while living on one income. So, he proposed something else: "I said, hey, this covers the whole country anyway, why don't I try working from home?"

Wood was game. She told him that it was totally against the rules and not to spread it around that he was doing a New York job from his home in Arizona, and that even her boss wouldn't know what they were up to. She was willing to give it a try, in no small part because she was desperate to have Hill on her team.

"Everything's easier," Wood told me, "if you're really a valuable employee."

Hill says working from home not only gave him more time with his family, but he also got more work done, too. An early riser, he typically rolled out of bed at five to work for a couple hours before the family got up at seven. The arrangement enabled him to keep the corporate job that he enjoyed, while also being at home with the kids when they got home after school, and participating in their daily routine.

"I really believe that we're wired, it's in our DNA to raise the next generation," says Hill, now a professor at Brigham Young University. "What I felt and resonated with is, as I was caring for these children—as I was changing their diapers and going for walks with them and feeding them and doing the day-to-day things—I was fulfilling a great purpose that resonated with me, and it was very satisfying. And I realized how much I had missed for the first ten or twelve years of my parenting career."

Hill's story is all the more impressive when you consider that he asked for his year off in 1987. There was no Skype, to say nothing of smartphones (or smart computers) and video conferencing. Telecommuting was a novel idea for all major corporations, not just IBM.

A few years later, when IBM was looking to save money anywhere they could, Hill was enlisted to help determine the viability of using telecommuting to save on real-estate costs. He conducted surveys with telecommuting employees and found that, on average, their performances were rated higher than their peers in the cubicle. Convinced that they could save not only money, but increase productivity, IBM engaged in a massive change to its corporate culture.

By 2009, more than 40 percent of IBM's 386,000 employees were without traditional offices. Since 1995, the company has sold 58 million square feet of office space for $1.9 billion, and subleased excess space for another billion dollars. Not having 40 percent of its workforce in the office saves the company more than $100 million a year.

* * *

The work/life balance landscape has changed a lot in the last two decades. The paternity leave stigma has begun to wear down and it's become trendy for companies to offer extended paternity leave: Netflix is offering up to a year, for example, and Facebook offers seventeen weeks. Of the 118 companies polled by Sheryl Sandberg's Lean In and McKinsey & Company in 2015, 65 percent offered extended maternity leave and 44 percent offered extended paternity leave. It gets better. They found that 85 percent of companies polled offered part-time opportunities and 82 percent offered telecommuting. Yet, aside from telecommuting, the other offerings are going untouched.

Two percent are taking employers up on part-time work. Only 1 percent of men are taking extended paternity leave and 4 percent of women take extended maternity leave. According to the study "more than 90 percent of both women and men believe taking extended family leave will hurt their careers."

And they have a point. In his years studying family leave, Scott Coltrane over at the University of Oregon has found the following to be true:

1. Taking extended leave can be one of the most rewarding experiences in a man's life.

2. Extended leave does take a long-term toll on your life-time earnings, whether you're a man or a woman.

Is that an acceptable risk for you?

* * *

I've traded a lot of money for time since I became a dad, and it's allowed me to do things I wouldn't have been able to do otherwise.

A few months ago, Thomas and I played hooky to bum around Seattle and go to a free festival at the Seattle Center, the hallowed grounds of the Space Needle, the Chihuly gift shop, and, every Labor Day weekend, Bumbershoot. When we got off the monorail, we noticed a playground surrounded by a blockade of cameras and a few hundred kids. We got close, right up against the yellow rope, and saw that the mayor and other city dignitaries were on hand for the grand opening.

I'd never seen a park like it. It's mostly rope netting situated in such a way that looks treacherous to kids and slyly safe to parents. At the center, an enclosed rope ladder with generous steps lead to a rope bridge that kids can walk on toward a large slide. This is Indiana Jones stuff. Nothing like we had.

When the ceremonial ribbon was cut, Thomas was among the hundreds of small bodies that rushed the new park. He waited in line to climb that ladder more patiently than I've ever seen him wait. When he started climbing, he gave me that familiar look of worry.

It's OK, buddy.

Keep climbing.

You'll be at the top soon.

It was one of those times when I could see my child hurtling toward something in his mind. When he got to the top, and started walking across the bridge toward the slide, I thought to myself: this is why I do what I do, why I've made the decisions that I've made.

One of the big surprises that I had while writing this book is meeting men who changed careers or made hard right turns to accommodate a different kind of life with their families. This isn't something I expected to see at all. In all of the instances, the men—writers, professors, taco vendors, and techies—have not only survived, but thrived. Putting their families first was their professional making.

It would be tempting for me to string these anecdotes together to make some kind of Gladwellian conclusion that putting your family first will put more money into your bank account, were it not that my own narrative keeps getting in the way.

After I got laid off from the *Weekly*, I made sure I posted links to my freelance work on Facebook, as much for my professional network as for my friends and family. I wanted the latter to know I was doing alright, and the former to know I was in the market for work and was, you know, working. But I've started to stop. Too many people tell me how well it seems that I was doing: you're writing for the *Wall Street Journal*! I saw your article in the inflight magazine on the way to Pittsburgh! Just this morning my cousin-in-law texted that he'd seen a piece of mine in *Maxim* while he watched his daughter get her haircut. "Pretty sweet man!" Makes me feel like a fraud.

The truth is that I worry that we're going to run out of money before Lucy's first birthday, that I go to bed every night wondering whether I'm being irresponsible.

I know I have other options, and I've explored them. But I don't get a responsible job at the bank because when I close my eyes and my vision is unobstructed, this is the path I see before me. I wake up in the morning and believe I'm in the right place, that what I'm doing is what's best for my family. It's not the financially responsible decision, but it is the one that feels best, for now, for our family.

Maybe someday soon that vision will change. Maybe there will come a time when I move back into the ranks of gainful employment with a regular paycheck, and maybe I'll go through financial hell to get there.

But even if everything falls apart tomorrow and I never get to play hooky on a school day again, I'll go to my grave grateful that I've seen the other side, that I know what it's like to report to a child rather than a boss, and that I was there the day Thomas became Indiana Jones.

Does that mean that dads who kiss their wife and kids good-bye before breakfast are callously handing over fatherhood chips for cash? Absolutely not.

But if you can't shake the feeling that you want to be doing something different, that the best thing for your family is to try something you've never seen done before, there are fewer excuses than there used to be to not give it a shot.

week 37

Take Studies, Recommendations, and (Especially) Books With a Grain of Salt

Your baby is about twenty-one inches long, from head to toe.

Your lady swears she can feel every inch. And is swearing more frequently.

The situation: Both of you are trying to keep track of all the recommendations and child-development studies you're seeing in your Facebook feed every day.

The reality: Not all recommendations and studies are created equal.

In the sixth week of the 2015/16 season, the Seahawks met the Carolina Panthers at home in Seattle hoping to revive their prospects of returning to a third straight Super Bowl, after opening the year with a pair of losses. A win against the Panthers would bring them back to even. By the fourth quarter things looked good. They were up 23 to 14 and all of the momentum was on their side of the ball. Until it wasn't.

Carolina scored a touchdown with 3:55 left in the game, and the extra point would close the gap to two. But Graham Gano missed the kick, and the Seahawks had been given a reprieve.

With the Hawks hanging onto a slim lead, I left Thomas asleep in my chair, Betsy on the couch with a bowl of popcorn, and Lucy scooting her eight-month-old body across the rug, to go downstairs to my office and call Dr. David Hill (a different Dr. David Hill than the former IBMer) to ask him whether the American Academy of Pediatrics recommended that we turn off the television.

"This is a great and classic question," said Dr. Hill, the chairperson of the AAP's council on communications and media. "Let's bring it back to what we know about young children and television."

As infants, they're developing their brains and their vocabulary. They pick up their words from their parents—not Russell Wilson—and when the television is on, the number of words per hour that they hear their parents speak drops from about 940 to 170. Additionally, the brains of infants and babies haven't developed to the point where they can fully comprehend what is taking place on a two-dimensional TV set. As such, the AAP recommends that children under the age of two should avoid TV and all screen time completely. This is an extreme recommendation for extreme conditions.

In homes where the TV is on all day every day, and kids are exposed to a constant barrage of Maury Povich and Jerry Springer, and they're not being spoken to and interacted with, they're hearing significantly fewer words come out of their parents' mouths than if the TV were off, and development is delayed. But, Dr. Hill said, "The TV itself is not poison. It's not like evil waves are going to come out of the TV and affect this child's brain."

"As a general rule, you'd like the TV off most of the time," he told me. "Does that mean you can't watch the Sunday afternoon football game and you're a bad parent for that? No. Of course, not."

This nuanced, commonsense approach was both surprising and unsurprising. It was unsurprising in that just about every time I ask an expert to explain a child-related policy or recommendation to me, the people invariably come across more nuanced and practical than the policy. But it was surprising because the AAP's recommendation—as articulated on the agency's parent-facing website, healthychildren.org—left no room for such reasonable accommodations as a baby being in the room while her parents watched a football game. It leaves so little wiggle room, in fact, that one of my friends told me that he's watched hardly any sports in the year since his son was born because his wife read that the AAP recommends that children under the age of two don't look at screens at all. This might seem petty, but when you're a new dad and not exactly killing it on the social scene, catching a game after work can be one of life's simple pleasures, which are snatched away by a literal interpretation of the recommendation.

Dr. Hill said that it's often the case with the agency's recommendations that "by the time these recommendations make it to a mainstream media outlet or to somebody's blog post or to a playdate, they have been frequently stripped of the nuance which the authors intended."

Speaking as a member of the media, I plead guilty to the notion that headlines don't always convey the full nuance of a study or debate. But I don't think the AAP is off the hook completely. After all, they do tell parents that "just having the TV on in the background, even if 'no one is watching it,' is enough to delay language development." *Yikes!*

But, making a larger point, Dr. Hill said that it's important for parents not to take in recommendations (even those made by the AAP) and the headlines of recent studies suggesting new reasons to worry about how you're raising a child without a critical eye, for several reasons.

First, there are two kinds of AAP recommendations. Some are based on better literature than others. "You don't have to have a degree in statistics to see that there have been dozens of randomized controlled trials that have all come up to the same result versus we collected some experts in a room and here's what they thought. Those are two very different kinds of evidence. A bunch of experts in a room are still frequently wrong. A bunch of randomized controlled trials that all come up to the same outcome are usually right."

Second, news organizations like reporting on the "wow" of every new study that comes along because it garners eyeballs and sells ads. "But, it also buys, sometimes, a false sense of hope or belief in products that aren't actually all that they're cracked up to be, or a false sense of fear of risks that aren't as scary as they may first seem."

Rather than get yourself worked up over every recommendation and study that gets pushed your way, Dr. Hill suggests that parents talk to their children's doctors to help them distinguish between what's really important—car seats, vaccines, infants sleeping on their backs—and what's not really important.

"As an environmentalist, for example, genetically modified foods are of great interest to me," he said. "I have some concerns over what these genes might do to our ecosystem. I have, on the other hand, almost no concerns over what these foods might do to my kids. The same is true for organic milk. I am worried about cows treated with antibiotics. I am not worried about whether the milk that my child drinks is organic. It is not, as far as I know, going to affect my child, which doesn't mean that I'm not concerned about some of the other issues surrounding factory farming. But that's not a big deal in terms of child health and well-being.

"Likewise, if your kid sits on your lap during the football game, that is not a big deal. If you keep daytime television on at all hours, that is a big deal."

Having blown the lead against the Panthers, the Seahawks are facing division rivals the 49ers in week seven and the very real prospect of going further in the hole than they have been in years. They're going to need every member of Hawks nation (the 12s!)— and every pound of eight-month-old Lucy—cheering them on. We'll all be watching.

Or, at least, scooting across the floor.

Week 38

A Small List for the Big Day

Your baby is done.

Your lady is done.

The situation: You're packing your bags.

The reality: Don't forget to pack a PowerBar (or two).

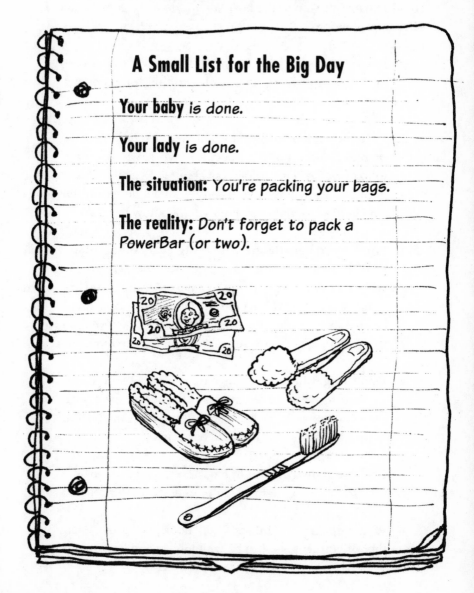

If you disregard every item on this list, you and your lady and your baby are going to be just fine. But, in case something here could make your stay in the hospital a little more comfortable, I offer the following:

1. **Preregister with your hospital.** If you went on a pre-birth tour, you probably already did this, but if not, get your crew preregistered.

2. **Write down her birth plan.** This will likely be part of preregistration, but it's good to have it because doctors/nurses will invariably ask about it. Even if the plan goes out the window, your lady will feel better on the way to the hospital knowing that you know her plan.

3. **Write down her allergies.** Seriously, every other person who walks into the room is going to ask her what meds she's allergic to. She's going to have other things on her mind, so be sure that you know all of them. And don't be shy about piping up—"She's allergic to X and Y"—when a nurse or doctor suggest she take something.

4. **Don't forget her overnight bag.** She's probably going to want to wear something she likes when she brings the baby home from the hospital (and the cameras are popping). Don't forget to grab her bag.

5. **Bring your own overnight bag.** You could be at the hospital for a couple nights. Don't forget your toothbrush.

6. **Pack slippers.** I think hospital floors are gross. Neither of you will want to be walking around barefoot in

there. But you might not want to keep your boots on for thirty-six hours, either. Pack slippers.

7. **Bring baby clothes.** You're going to be bringing a baby home from the hospital, so don't forget to bring her some clothes!

8. **Bring cash.** As I mentioned before, when Thomas was born, I had to pay for all *my* meals in the hospital room with cash. I ran out pretty quick and had to ask my dad to bring me some. He was happy to do so, and it wasn't a big deal, but "bring me a handful of twenties" is usually not the kind of thing people mean when they ask what they can do to help.

9. **Clear your phone.** You're going to feel like a fool when you go to take your first picture of your son and your iPhone is full. Clear out as much as you can before you go to the hospital, because I have a feeling you're going to have a few pictures to take. And, yeah, don't forget your charger.

10. **Pack some food.** I made the mistake of going down to the cafeteria while Betsy was in labor with Thomas—she said it was OK! —and when I came back half the hospital had descended on her room (it turned out fine). Stay close. Pack enough snacks to get you through twelve or twenty-four hours. Just make sure that whatever it is doesn't smell like something that will make her retch.

week 39

A Small List for the Next Day

Your baby is in the batter's box.

Your lady has put her swollen feet up.

The situation: You've put your feet up.

The reality: That's good. Get some rest. But try to get a head start on tomorrow, too.

*T*wo days after Thomas was born was the only time in my life I can honestly remember not knowing what day of the week it was. We were in the waiting room before his first posthospital doctor's appointment, and I was trying to hold down a conversation with a sweet little girl and her mother.

> **Sweet Little Girl:** What's his name?
> **Me:** Thomas.
> **Sweet Little Girl:** Oh, he's really going to like Thomas the train.
> **Her Mother:** What day was he born?
> **Me:** Two days ago. What is today?
> **Betsy:** Chris, did you bring the diaper bag?
> **Me:** No. Did you?
> **Betsy:** No.

By the time you get back from the hospital, you're going to be an exhausted basket of excitement and joy. Both of you will have been up for the better part of forty-eight hours. You're going to forget things. Betsy and I didn't even bring the diaper bag to Thomas's first doctor's appointment. Because your brain won't be firing on all cylinders, do yourself a favor and have a few of the basics worked out before you get home. Here are a few places to start:

1. **Pack the diaper bag.** Bringing the diaper bag won't do any good if it's not packed. As long as you've got some diapers, rags, wipes, sanitizer, and whatever tools you need for feeding—depending on your method of feeding, of course—you'll be fine.

2. **Stock up on food.** Your friends and well-wishers aren't necessarily going to have casseroles delivered to you as soon as you come home with the baby, since ETAs vary greatly. So, have enough food in the house to get you through a couple days so you don't have to make unnecessary trips to the grocery story. As my grandma always says: you can put a frozen roast in the Crock-Pot in the morning and have it for dinner. So, yeah, throw a few roasts (or whatever you're eating) in the freezer. And say yes to all offered meals. But be sure you're both fed. I ran a little late bringing Mexican food over to my friends' house a couple days after they had their first baby. She was starving, so he quickly went out and grabbed her food, and got home ten minutes before I showed up. Any other time a friend is bringing you food, this is rude. Here, it is commendable behavior. Get her fed. Don't worry about being polite. And put the tardy tamales in the fridge for breakfast (best breakfast ever).

3. **Who's helping?** I'm in the "take whatever help you can get" camp, but there are several considerations. If your lady doesn't want to see people, don't be shy about keeping people away. And, yes, it's your job to tell people they can't come over to "help." Don't make your lady do it. At the same time, when people say, "If there's anything I can do let me know," don't be shy about telling them that it would be a big help for them to come over a week after the baby's born to help you pick up the house and/or watch the sleeping baby while you and your lady take showers. People like to be helpful. I also think it's a good idea to have a couple friends on retainer who will agree to be on call for errands. You'll

feel better about calling your buddy to ask him to run to the grocery store for you if you've told him in advance that you'll be calling him for quick errands. Speaking as someone who has no practical skills to offer family and friends, I love it when it turns out that I can be helpful.

4. **What are your safe words?** Exhaustion and sleep deprivation can do wild things to people. Everyone gets whittled down to nothing from time to time and needs a break. Andrew Smiler, the couples' therapist, told me that he and his wife will actually call each other on particularly stressful days to tag out. He recommends couples set up code words to use with each other, since there's a big difference between "I could use an extra set of hands" and "I'm so frustrated I feel like I could hit the kid." Set up a code word for when one of you needs an immediate break.

5. **Who's doing what?** When she gets home from the hospital, she's going to be recovering from a rather traumatic physical experience (and possibly surgery/procedure). She's not going to be able to do all the household duties she normally does. Figure out which of those things you can pick up, and tell her in advance you'll be doing them so she can chillax and feel good about napping with the baby. Also, decide as a couple what is acceptable to *not* do for a week or two (vacuuming, mowing the lawn, etc.) and don't stress about them not getting done.

weeks 40 to 947

No Child Has Ever Been Brought Up Right

Your baby is amazing.

Your lady is fantastic.

The situation: You're doing the best that you can, but you worry that it's not enough.

The reality: Remember what Jimmy Stewart said in the classic family comedy, *Mr. Hobbs Takes a Vacation:* "In the whole history of the world there's never been a child brought up right."

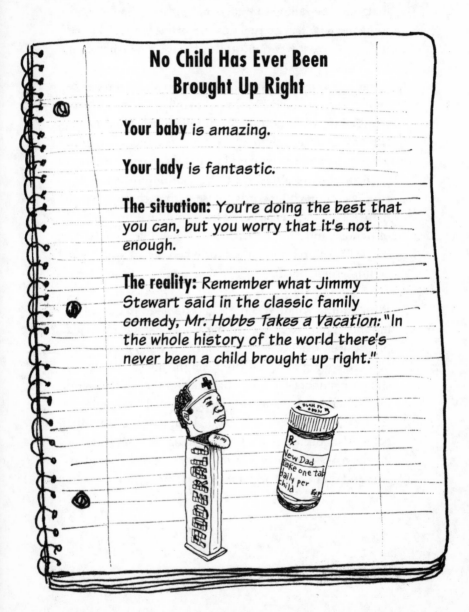

I've always been into grilling. And I've always been partial to charcoal.

It's not that I don't like gas grills or see the convenience. I prefer charcoal to gas for the same reason you prefer vinyl to CD: I like the ritual. I like cleaning my Weber, scraping the grate, filling a chimney with newspaper and charcoal, then watching it burn while I sip a drink in the half-broken Adirondack chair we got when we bought our house.

When Thomas got around to his second birthday, the ritual changed.

Thomas likes charcoal, too. He doesn't know about gas grills. He doesn't know how easy it is to push a button and get grill-ready heat in a minute and a half. This is proof, once again, that I've deprived my child of the best life possible. But he's not complaining. When he's in the mood for a well-seared burger, we head outside together.

He picks his own piece of newspaper to crumple, and prefers ones with colorful pictures. He fetches loose coals when I shake 'em out of the bag. He likes to help clean out the old ashes. And he likes to be the one who chucks them into the trash.

I haven't given up the beverage part of the ritual completely, but there's far less sitting around than there used to be. These days, when we're waiting for the coals to burn, we have pinecone fights or play soccer on our back lawn that's actually a small hill (yes, the ball ends up at the bottom on every other kick—again, this child is deprived).

I'd like to say that our days are all like this, that it's always a merry scene with a happy kid helping dad put food on the table. But that's a fantasy.

We're not always at our best. We all let ourselves down. We all fall short.

I'll never forget one particularly frustrating evening when Thomas just wouldn't stay in bed. When he came out of his bedroom for what had to have been the tenth time, I couldn't take it anymore.

Just lay down.

Let your eyes rest.

You'll fall asleep if you let yourself.

Do not *get out of bed again.*

I love you.

Goodnight.

No sooner had I left the room did I hear him stir.

That's it!

I swung open the door—slammed open, if that's possible—in that dramatic "I gotcha! Caught you red-handed!" kind of way. It scared Thomas. He was in no danger of being hit by the door, but I could tell that the force of my conviction and the shock of my uncorked frustration felt like a body-blow to my three-year-old.

He stood there, startled, scared, and started to sniffle. He tried to explain himself, but got caught up in a cry. He tried to tell me what was wrong. I didn't even notice that he was no longer wearing his pajamas. He pointed to his fleece footie PJs on the floor, and as he cried, the only words I could make out were "too hot."

* * *

I've never been to see a psychiatrist for, I don't know, a session, to talk about what I've been up to. But for a while, I had to go see a psychiatrist every three months to get my Adderall. It was a painless, pointless, five-minute meeting in which he asked me how things were going, and I told him "fine." He wrote me a prescription and a couple hundred dollars were exchanged between me, my insurance company, and my PEZ-loving shrink.

Once, I decided to go with it, to actually tell him how things were going. I told him I was tired. That I felt like I wasn't being a very good dad. That I was snapping at my son. That I was worried that I was scarring him for life.

I was hoping I could get up on the couch a bit. Get my money's worth. But I couldn't get him to give me an hour. He bought me off with "kids are resilient."

Sure, I (or my insurance company) had to pay a hundred bucks a word for his advice, but he's right. Kids are resilient. Kids are impossibly, inspiringly forgiving. Kids turn out well, even when they're not treated optimally 100 percent of the time, even when the people charged, overjoyed to care for them fall short.

Dr. Jim Griffin at the National Institutes of Health put it to me this way: "Kids are really pretty resilient creatures, from birth on up. Obviously, when they're infants they require a lot of care. But even then, they're sometimes more resilient and they're learning a lot more than we give them credit for. The research certainly bears that out."

You're gonna get tired. You're gonna lose your patience. You're going to get mad. You're going to make mistakes. We all do. Don't be afraid that you've ruined your child.

* * *

A couple years ago, Thomas and I stepped up our game. I found a vintage, electric smoker with a seventies-orange paint job at a rummage sale, and was elated to bring it home and discover that it worked.

Thomas and I immediately started doing our homework. We scoured Google and YouTube for meat-smoking brilliance. Eventually, we found our way to a public television series hosted by Aaron Franklin, a dude about my age who is the owner of the massively popular Austin restaurant, Franklin Barbecue.

When we found Franklin's series, we knew we'd found our guru. Franklin taught us how to select a brisket, how to make a rub, how to trim the fat. He's fond of giving instructions of the "you could do this, but if you don't, it's not a big deal" variety; things like: "Just trim until you're sick of trimming." If you don't do it all, it's not a big deal because, "eh, it's barbecue." That's because barbecue is forgiving. You're smoking large pieces of meat that will cook for a very long time—twelve hours if you're doing a brisket his way.

The thing is, we don't have a wood-fired smoker like Franklin. We can't even get the whole brisket into our smoker. We have to cut it in half. Worse, we're supposed to be smoking the meat between 225 and 250 degrees. But in the last eighteen months, I've never been able to get that damn thing over 170.

So, we have to improvise. We put our meat on at night. I add wood chunks until I can't stay awake any longer, and revisit things in the morning. Then I take the meat out of the smoker, wrap it in tin foil and—horror of all horrors!—put it in the oven for a few hours to bring it up to temperature. And it tastes wonderful.

I don't always do all the things that Franklin suggests. I don't always let the meat rest for an hour after cooking, sometimes I spread too much rub on the roast, and I've used ketchup with *high fructose corn syrup* to make my sauce. I do what I can with the tools, time, and energy that I have. It's not perfect. It's never going to be perfect.

After a year of using the Aaron Franklin method of barbecue as my base, I caught up with the chef for a story I was working on. During our interview, he told me his wife had recently given birth to a little girl. As we were wrapping things up, I bounced a theory off him: was parenting at all like barbecue? He was right there with me.

"I was just telling someone the other day that parenting is like barbecue. You try your best, and when things don't work out you work them out together."

* * *

As I was interviewing people for this book, I often finished by presenting them with the following scenario: you're sitting on an airplane, a man sits down next to you, and the two of you strike up a conversation. It turns out that he's about to become a father. He wants to know what advice you have. What are the first words that come out of your mouth? Answers varied, but almost all of them centered around the same theme. Here's a sampling:

> Hold that baby as much as you can and be in the moment with that baby, and make faces and connect and do crazy things. The baby will teach you what to do. Just do things that make the baby smile. Kids are only infants once. If there's an option to trade money for time, take a little bit of extra time, especially during that first year, to really bond with your infant.
>
> —*Dr. Jeff Hill, Brigham Young University's School of Family Life*

> When you've finished a hard day at work and you're sitting down and your child wants to show you something or read you something or explain something to you or they want you to read them a story, and you're a bit too tired and you want to go off and do something else and maybe watch your own TV show or go sit and have a beer, do the thing that your child wants you to do. Because there will come a time when they no longer want to ask you about those sorts of things. And then you'll be thinking, Oh, you don't ask me to do these things anymore. Make the most of it when you can, because it is fleeting, like the rest of life.
>
> —*Paul Franklin, the Oscar-winning visual effect supervisor behind* Interstellar

Enjoy it. It is an emotional rollercoaster. Sleep deprivation gets to you, but the newborn period is a relatively short period in your life. A lot of people are just sort of struggling to get through it and don't realize how quickly that part is over. Know that, yeah, it's going to be a really busy period initially, but there's so many rewards out of it.

—*Dr. Judy Kimelman, OB/GYN*

Have fun. Really seek to be happy. Tune out the bad stuff. That's the whole thing in terms of having a rich life, is learning how to make yourself happy, learning how to make your partner happy. Children are supposed to be a source of joy. Have fun is the number one thing.

—*Dr. Susan Lemagie, OB/GYN*

None of them suggest reading a bounty of literature. None of them recommend a method of parenting. None of them told a cautionary tale. You may not feel ready to be a dad. You may feel overwhelmed. But the secret to raising kids isn't amassing vast amounts of knowledge and skills and knowing exactly what to do during every conceivable scenario that could arise.

I believe it's about what Dr. Keyes says: "If the child feels loved and accepted and listened to, then everything else will fall into place."

Good luck.

Postscript

So, there you go, you've had nine months to learn how to take care of a baby by taking care of a pregnant woman, and the better part of a year to clean yourself up. How'd you do?

Not perfect yet? For shame!

That's OK. Sometimes it takes longer than nine months to get clean. Remember my porn-addicted friend, Bryce? He told his wife that he'd give it up by the time the baby was born. But it wasn't until she was pregnant with their second child that he finally started going to Sex Addicts Anonymous and got clean.

Me? I've done alright. I could be doing better. In fact, lately I feel like I've been slipping. This morning, for example, I stayed in bed, half-asleep when I heard Lucy calling for me from her crib.

Thomas was the first one by her side. You know you've let yourself go when your four-year-old is more attuned to the needs of your infant than you are.

I eventually got out of bed, walked into Lucy's room, and saw Thomas on the floor—his favorite stuffed puppy in his arms—entertaining his sister with glow sticks and a Halloween snowman through the bars of her crib. I sat down next to him and joined the party.

Thomas proclaimed that Lucy seemed like she needed a puppy of her own. Without having to think about it, he reached into a bin next to her crib and fished out the stuffed animal he'd picked out for her at IKEA. If I had been left looking for the puppy on my own, I would have embarrassed myself as much as I did the night before, when I had to text Betsy and ask her where we keep the screwdriver.

Betsy got a bottle ready and fed Lucy in the living room while Thomas and I played in the dark with the gift pack of glowing objects his grandma sent him for Halloween.

A few minutes later, Thomas asked me—completely out of the blue—if adults lied.

Only to protect you, I thought to myself.

Thomas doesn't need to know everything. For example, after I was feeling smug and in control of my bodily functions in the years after he was born, I decided to tempt fate and, you know, enjoy the benefits of drawer-free living for a while. One day when Thomas was, well, I don't know the exact age—still napping in the afternoon is as close as I can get it—my friend Vince came over to hang out.

When it was time for Thomas to hang it up for the afternoon, we excused ourselves, went to his bedroom, and started to read books. After sitting on the floor for ten minutes, I started to get up and, in a single motion, bend over to tuck Thomas into bed. Except it wasn't a single motion. It was many motions—one, in particular, in a place from which I wasn't hoping for any movement.

This was complicated, obviously. I hadn't sung Thomas any songs yet, so he wasn't going to fall asleep. And Vince was in the living room watching TV. I had to come up with lies for them both.

Thomas was fairly easy to manipulate. I bought him off by telling him I had to go to the bathroom, a lie by omission, sure, but by parenting standards, I was Honest Abe.

Vince, actually, didn't need any explaining, either. He didn't seem to notice that I emerged from my bedroom wearing different pants. Then again, I've seen Vince wear two different shoes in public, so I don't think he's too bothered by what people around him are wearing.

I went back into Thomas's room, tucked him in, sang "If All the Raindrops" and "Itsy Bitsy Spider," gave him a kiss, and shut the door. He never suspected a thing.

The infallibility of fatherhood is not a bubble I'm going to burst for my son any time soon. I'm not going to volunteer that I'm not gainfully employed and that I don't have this life thing figured out. And I'm not going to tell him what happened to my favorite pair of jeans.

If you don't feel like you're ready for the whole fatherhood thing just yet, relax. Give it your best. Don't beat yourself up.

And, for heaven's sake, don't shit yourself.

Acknowledgments

I count among the great blessings of my life that I never went to bed wondering if I would be cared for in the morning and that every day I felt loved, accepted, and listened to. It's something I took for granted until I reached a level of understanding that what I grew up with was not a given. It wasn't until years later that I learned that my parents had anxieties and financial worries of their own at my age.

So, thank you, Mom and Dad, for your love, attention, and enthusiasm and for sheltering me from said worries. And, sorry, Lucy and Thomas, for spilling all of mine for you to see when you're old enough to read and interested enough in what I have to say to read it. Here's hoping the circles in that Venn diagram don't intersect for a couple more decades. But whenever it does, thank you for reading, thank you for giving me material, and thank you for your patience and love on a level that I am still learning to appreciate.

To Simon and Mason: perhaps my only true regret (and I don't think that's really the right word) in my life as a parent is that neither Thomas nor Lucy will know what it's like to have brothers (plural). It's been a great ride. I love you both.

Thank you, Aaron Bagley, for figuring out a way to bring levity and heft to this project while juggling Baxter with your left hand and a glass of gin with your right. Thanks, as well, to Jessixa and Baxter for making him available and keeping him awesome.

Thank you, Duff, for teaching me many things about parenting and punctuation. I should never have questioned the fact that GN'R has but one apostrophe.

Thank you to my good friend Mark Fefer, who patiently considers each of my get-rich slow schemes and was especially encouraging of this one. Thank you, Shawn O'Neal, for your lessons, ticks, and original clichés. Thank you, Mike Seely, my friend and favorite writer of creative nonfiction.

Thank you, Soumeya Bendimerad Roberts, for taking an idea and figuring out how to turn it into a book. Without your early edits and encouragement, fatherhood would rock, but it would not be read.

Thank you to everyone at Da Capo Press and Lifelong Books, especially my editor, Dan Ambrosio, and my friend Ben Schafer.

Thank you, Leah Sottile, for your early reads and ideas.

Thank you, Erin Bamer, for your accuracy and proficiency.

Thank you, Gwen Elliott, for always knowing where to find a good can downtown.

For your advice, encouragement (and the occasional paycheck), thank you, David Ritz, Charles Cross, Brian Gallagher, Michael Hsu, Jim Morgan, Dan Mandel, Chris Barron, David Nelson, Daniel Wattenberg, John J. Edwards III, Chuck Strouse, Deirdra Funcheon, Sarah Elbert, Daniel Pearson, Paul DeBarros, Andy Hermann, Vince Dice, David Symonds, Chad Lewis, Cole Childers, Brian Smith, Bill Denton, Tony Bonuccelli, Joel Pals, Brian Harper, Chelsea Tennyson, and Tyler Tennyson.

And, of course, thank you to Betsy. For everything. Especially the baby-making. I love you. I love you. I love you.

Notes

Week 5: You Don't "Need" a Bigger Place

6 **Your baby's heart is beginning to beat:** Keith A. Eddleman and Joanne Stone, *The New Pregnancy Bible*, 4th ed. (London: Carrol & Brown Ltd., 2013), 31.

Week 6: Hang Onto Your Stereo and Record Collection

11 **Your baby has a brain:** Eddleman and Stone, *The New Pregnancy Bible*, 31.

11 **Your lady is nauseous:** Glade B. Curtis and Judith Schuler, *Your Pregnancy Week By Week*, 6th ed. (Boston: Da Capo Press, 2008), 100.

Week 7: In Defense of Selling Out

25 **"At some point you need to have a bunch of kids":** James C. McKinley Jr., "Former Busker Is Now Back as a Solo," *New York Times*, June 24, 2012.

Week 8: What to Expect When She's Reading *What to Expect*

26 **Your baby is the size of a pinto bean:** Curtis and Schuler, *Your Pregnancy Week By Week*, 130.

29 **For example, performing oral sex on a pregnant woman:** Jodi Kantor, "Expecting Trouble: The Book They Love to Hate," *New York Times*, September 15, 2005, http://www.nytimes.com/2005/09/15/fashion/thursdaystyles/expecting-trouble-the-book-they-love-to-hate.html?_r=0.

Week 9: Ask Her What You Can Be Doing Better

30 **Your baby is starting to look like a human being:** Curtis and Schuler, *Your Pregnancy Week By Week*, 145.

31 **During the first trimester, when women aren't showing:** Laura Veirs (musician), in discussion with the author, March 24, 2015.

Week 10: Respect Yourself: Don't Carry a Diaper Bag

33 **Your baby has officially graduated from embryo to fetus:** Eddleman and Stone, *The New Pregnancy Bible*, 33.

33 **Your lady has a uterus the size of a grapefruit:** "Week 10," BabyCenter.com, http://www.babycenter.com/6_your -pregnancy-10-weeks_1099.bc.

Week 12: Lose Weight Before the Sympathy Weight (Otherwise, Buy a Vest)

44 **Your baby is putting on weight—he's up to a half ounce:** Eddleman and Stone, *The New Pregnancy Bible*, 35.

44 **Your lady is beginning to get over her morning sickness:** Eddleman and Stone, *The New Pregnancy Bible*, Your Pregnant Body chart.

Week 13: Fight for the Fatherhood You Want for Your Family

47 **Your baby is the size of a peach:** Curtis and Schuler, *Your Pregnancy Week By Week*, 198.

47 **Your lady has tender breasts:** "Week 13," www.whattoexpect .com, http://www.whattoexpect.com/pregnancy/week-by -week/week-13.aspx.

Week 14: Watch Out for Depression

58 **Your baby weighs about an ounce and a half:** Growth Chart: Fetal Length and Weight, Week By Week, http://www .babycenter.com/average-fetal-length-weight-chart.

59   **Many women get and get over the baby blues in the two
      weeks after birth:** American Pregnancy Association,
      http://americanpregnancy.org/first-year-of-life/baby-blues/.

59   **Between 14 and 23 percent of women get depressed during
      pregnancy:** The American College of Obstetricians and
      Gynecologists, http://www.acog.org/About-ACOG/News
      -Room/News-Releases/2009/Depression-During-Pregnancy.

59   **Between 8 and 19 percent report frequent depressive
      symptoms after birth:** Centers for Disease Control and
      Prevention, http://www.cdc.gov/reproductivehealth
      /depression/.

59   **Depression symptoms during pregnancy:** Sonia Murdock
      (cofounder and executive director of the Postpartum Resource
      Center of New York), in discussion with the author, June 19, 2015.

Week 15: Don't Let Her Microwave Bologna

62   **Your baby has started sucking his thumb:** Curtis and Schuler,
      Your Pregnancy Week By Week, 227.

63   **Pregnant women . . . are ten times more likely to get
      listeriosis:** Centers for Disease Control and Prevention, 2013,
      http://www.cdc.gov/listeria/risk.html.

63   **The Centers for Disease Control and Prevention estimate that
      1,600 people will get listeriosis:** Centers for Disease Control
      and Prevention, 2014, http://www.cdc.gov/listeria/statistics
      .html.

63   **Almost four million births in the United States in 2013:**
      Centers for Disease Control and Prevention, 2013,
      http://www.cdc.gov/nchs/fastats/births.htm.

64   **A man's chance of getting breast cancer is 1 in 1000:** "What are
      the key statistics about breast cancer in men?," cancer.org, 2015,
      http://www.cancer.org/cancer/breastcancerinmen
      /detailedguide/breast-cancer-in-men-key-statistics.

64   **The American Academy of Pediatrics declared that "no
      amount of alcohol intake should be considered safe" during
      pregnancy:** Janet F. Williams, Vincent C. Smith, Janet F.
      Williams, and the Committee on Substance Abuse, "Clinical

Report: Fetal Alcohol Spectrum Disorders," *Pediatrics* (October 19, 2015), http://pediatrics.aappublications.org/content/early/2015/10/13/peds.2015–3113.full.pdf+html.

64 **Numerous studies through the years have observed that a couple drinks a week had no effect on babies:** Leiv S. Bakketeig et al., "Low to Moderate Average Alcohol Consumption and Binge Drinking in Early Pregnancy: Effects on Choice Reaction Time and Information Processing Time in Five-Year-Old Children," *PLOS ONE* (September 18, 2015), http://journals.plos.org/plosone/article?id=10.1371/journal.pone.0138611; Ron Gray et al., "Light drinking in pregnancy, a risk for behavioural problems and cognitive deficits at 3 years of age?" *The International Journal of Epidemiology* (August 2015), http://ije.oxfordjournals.org/content/38/1/129.

65 **Omega-3 fatty acids found in fish:** Emily Oster, "Approval Matrix," *Expecting Better* (New York: Penguin Press, 2013), 86, 88.

Week 16: Having a Baby Doesn't Change Everything

66 **Your baby is moving enough that your lady might notice:** Curtis and Schuler, *Your Pregnancy Week By Week*, 240.

Week 17: Yes, Swaddling Is a Sport

75 **Your baby is starting to put on some fat:** Eddleman and Stone, *The New Pregnancy Bible*, 37.

75 **Your lady is starting to have some creative food cravings:** Eddleman and Stone, *The New Pregnancy Bible*, Your Pregnant Body chart.

Week 18: Shush Your Way to the Happiest Baby on the Block

79 **Your baby is the size of a sweet potato; Your lady has put on a dozen pounds:** http://www.whattoexpect.com/pregnancy/week-by-week/week-18.aspx.

Week 19: You Can Take It With You

82   **Your baby weighs eight and a half ounces:** Growth Chart: Fetal Length and Weight, Week By Week, http://www.babycenter. com/average-fetal-length-weight-chart.

83   **The Mariners . . . had lost four out of their last five:** Baseball-Reference.com, http://www.baseball-reference.com /boxes/SEA/SEA199508240.shtml.

88   **That win, that home run, has been credited:** Larry Stone, "Top moments from an unforgettable 1995 Mariners season," *Seattle Times*, August 24, 2015, http://www.seattletimes.com/sports /mariners/top-moments-from-an-unforgettable-1995-mariners -season/.

Week: 21: Listen to Caspar Babypants

96   **Your baby has taste buds:** Eddleman and Stone, *The New Pregnancy Bible*, 40.

Week 22: It's OK: Nobody Else Knows How They're Going to Make It Work, Either

100   **Your baby has fully-formed eyelids and eyebrows:** Curtis and Schuler, *Your Pregnancy Week By Week*, 323.

103   **A 2006 study put out by the National Institutes of Health's National Institute of Child Health and Human Development:** "The NICHD Study of Early Child Care and Youth Development," US Department of Health and Human Services, 2006, https://www.nichd.nih.gov/publications/pubs/ documents/seccyd_06.pdf.

Week 23: You Can Do Better, Even If You've Never Seen It Done Before

113   **Your baby weighs about a pound:** Curtis and Schuler, *Your Pregnancy Week By Week*, 338.

Week 24: You Can't Properly Install a Car Seat
Unless You've Seen It Done Before

119   **Your baby has a face, and it's filling out:** "Week 24,"
      whattoexpect.com, http://www.whattoexpect.com/pregnancy
      /week-by-week/week-24.aspx.

121   **When the National Highway Traffic Safety Administration
      conducted a study:** "Drivers' Mistakes When Installing
      Child Seats," US Department of Transportation National
      Highway Traffic Safety Administration, No. DOT HS 811 234
      (Dec. 2009).

Week 25: Consider the Formula

124   **Your baby is already growing adult teeth:** Eddleman and
      Stone, *The New Pregnancy Bible*, 43.

129   **A 2014 study of mothers in the U.K. showed that women at
      the highest risk of postpartum depression were the ones who
      had planned to breast-feed but were unable to.:** Cristina Borra,
      Maria Iacovou, and Almudena Sevilla, "New Evidence on
      Breastfeeding and Postpartum Depression: The Importance of
      Understanding Women's Intentions," *Maternal and Child Health
      Journal* 19 (April 2015), http://link.springer.com/content
      /pdf/10.1007%2Fs10995–014–1591-z.pdf.

132   **The World Health Organization recommends exclusive
      breast-feeding:** "Infant and young child feeding," World
      Health Organization Media Centre, July 2015,
      http://www.who.int/mediacentre/factsheets/fs342/en/.

132   **In a 2001 study published in the *Journal of the American
      Medical Association*:** Michal S. Kramer et al., "Promotion of
      Breastfeeding Intervention Trial," *The Journal of the American
      Medical Association* (January 24/31 2001), http://jama.
      jamanetwork.com/article.aspx?articleid=193490#RESULTS.

132   **A Dutch study that's cited in the AAP's statement on breast-
      feeding compared exclusively breast-fed infants with those
      who had never been breast-fed:** Liesbeth Duijts et al.,

"Prolonged and Exclusive Breastfeeding Reduces the Risk of
Infectious Diseases in Infancy," *Pediatrics* (June 21, 2010),
http://pediatrics.aappublications.org/content/126/1/e18.

133 The authors of a 2001 study published in the *Journal of the
American Medical Association*: Mary L. Hediger et al.,
"Association Between Infant Breastfeeding and Overweight in
Young Children," *Journal of the American Medical Association*
(May 16, 2001), http://jama.jamanetwork.com/article.aspx
?articleid=193838.

133 "The evidence suggests that for every six children": David
Meyers, "Breastfeeding and Health Outcomes," *Breastfeeding
Medicine* (October 4, 2009), http://www.ncbi.nlm.nih.gov
/pmc/articles/PMC2998971/.

134 AAP: "Feeding your infant provides more than just good
nutrition.": Healthychildren.org, American Academy of
Pediatrics, 2015, https://www.healthychildren.org/English
/ages-stages/baby/breastfeeding/Pages/default.aspx.

134 Susan G. Komen for the Cure puts the risk of women in the
United States getting breast cancer: www.komen.org, 2015,
http://ww5.komen.org/BreastCancer/UnderstandingRisk
.html.

134 Komen cites a study that shows that "mothers who breast-fed":
The Lancet Publishing Group, "Collaborative Group on
Hormonal Factors in Breast Cancer. Breast cancer and breast
feeding: collaborative reanalysis of individual data from
47 epidemiological studies in 30 countries, including 50,302
women with breast cancer and 96,973 women without the
disease," 2002 , http://www.ncbi.nlm.nih.govpubmed/12133652.

134 Komen says that "women who give birth for the first time
after age 35": http://ww5.komen.org/KomenPerspectives
/Does-pregnancy-affect-breast-cancer-risk-and-survival-.html.

135 "It's only free if a woman's time is worth nothing": Hanna
Rosin, "The Case Against Breast-Feeding," *The Atlantic*, April
2009, http://www.theatlantic.com/magazine/archive
/2009/04/the-case-against-breast-feeding/307311/.

135 **The AAP says: "Research also suggests that breast-feeding may help":** Healthychildren.org, American Academy of Pediatrics, 2015,https://www.healthychildren.org/English /ages-stages/baby/breastfeeding/Pages/Why-Breastfeed .aspx.

136 **"One of the well-known confounders in breast-feeding research is demographic difference":** Mei Chung et al., "A Summary of the Agency for Healthcare Research and Quality's Evidence Report on Breastfeeding in Developed Countries," *Breastfeeding Medicine* 4:1 (2009), http://www.ncbi.nlm.nih .gov/pubmed/19827919.

136 **Cynthia G. Colen and David M. Ramey compared children who had been breast-fed with siblings who had been formula-fed:** Cynthia G. Colen and David M. Ramey, "Is Breast Truly Best? Estimating the Effects of Breastfeeding on Long-term Child Health and Wellbeing in the United States Using Sibling Comparisons," *Social Science & Medicine* (May 2014), http://www.sciencedirect.com/science/journal/02779536/109.

Week 26: Pick a Pediatrician You Actually Like

138 **Your baby has developed all five senses:** Curtis and Schuler, *Your Pregnancy Week By Week*, 379.

Week 27: Don't Be Afraid to Be an Asshole

142 **Your baby is the size of an eggplant; your lady has swollen ankles:** whattoexpect.com, http://www.whattoexpect.com /pregnancy/week-by-week/week-27.aspx.

Week 28: Walk, Don't Run:
Giving Birth Isn't Like It Is On TV

147 **Your baby baby has crossed the two-pound mark:** Curtis and Schuler, *Your Pregnancy Week By Week*, 408.

Week 29: You Don't Need a Six-Week
Birthing Course (Only a 3x5 Card)

153   **Your baby is up to two and a half pounds:** "Growth Chart,"
      babycenter.com.

153   **Your lady may be dealing with varicose veins on her legs:**
      Eddleman and Stone, *The New Pregnancy Bible*, Your Pregnant
      Body chart.

Week 30: But, of Course, Take the Birthing Course

158   **Your baby is about sixteen inches long:** "Growth Chart,"
      babycenter.com.

Week 31: Just Do Everything Yourself

161   **Your baby is hiccupping:** whattoexpect.com, http://www.
      whattoexpect.com/pregnancy/week-by-week/week-31.aspx.

161   **Your lady is a bit more forgetful than usual:** Eddleman and
      Stone, *The New Pregnancy Bible*, Your Pregnant Body chart.

Week 32: Make Time for the Two of You

164   **Your baby sleeps more than 90 percent of the day:** Eddleman
      and Stone, *The New Pregnancy Bible*, 46.

Week 33: Forget the Garden, Get a Crock-Pot

169   **Your baby weighs about four and a half pounds; your lady
      has put on about five times that:** Curtis and Schuler, *Your
      Pregnancy Week By Week*, 477.

172   **"Back when many of us were growing up, we led lives that
      kept most of us at a pretty healthy weight,":** Michelle Obama,
      "Why I'm Fighting Childhood Obesity," *Newsweek*, March 13,
      2010, http://www.newsweek.com/michelle-obama-why-im
      -fighting-childhood-obesity-69655.

172 **In 2012 . . . both parents were working outside the home:**
     "Employment characteristics of families," The Economics Daily,
     Bureau of Labor Statistics, US Department of Labor,
     http://www.bls.gov/opub/ted/2013/ted_20130430.htm.

173 **In 1975, when Mrs. Obama was ten years old:** US Congress
     Joint Economic Committee, "How Working Mothers Contribute
     to the Economic Security of American Families," May 2015,
     http://www.jec.senate.gov/public/_cache/files/8dbdedb8
     -b41d-484c-b702-9269fcf37c9b/jec-mothers-day.pdf.

Week 34: Free Time Isn't a Luxury. It's a Necessity.

176 **Your baby is the size of a honeydew:** whattoexpect.com,
     http://www.whattoexpect.com/pregnancy/week-by-week
     /week-34.aspx.

Week 35: There Will Be a Parent Running Point
(The Other One Is Helping)

182 **Your baby has put his head down for evacuation:** Eddleman
     and Stone, *The New Pregnancy Bible*, 47.

182 **Your lady's feet no longer fit into her tennis shoes.** Curtis and
     Schuler, *Your Pregnancy Week By Week*, 505.

Week 36: To Paternity Leave (and Beyond!)

186 **Your baby is in her sixth pound:** Curtis and Schuler, *Your
     Pregnancy Week By Week*, 515.

190 **By 2009, more than 40 percent of IBM's 386,000 employees
     were without traditional offices:** Janet Caldow, "Working
     Outside the Box: A Study of the Growing Momentum in
     Telework," Institute for Electronic Government, IBM
     Corporation, January 21, 2009, http://www-01.ibm.com
     /industries/government/ieg/pdf/working_outside_the
     _box.pdf.

190 **Netflix is offering up to a year of paid paternity leave:** Kylie Gumpert, "Netflix's year-long parental leave raises bar for US employers," *Reuters*, August 5, 2015, http://www.reuters.com /article/2015/08/05us-netflix-maternity-idUSKCN0QA298 20150805.

190 **Facebook offers 17 weeks of paternity leave:** Akane Otani, "The 10 U.S. Companies With the Best Paternity Leave Benefits," Bloomberg.com, April 30, 2015, http://www.bloomberg.com/news/articles/2015–04–30 /the-10-u-s-companies-with-the-best-paternity-leave-benefits.

190 **Of the 118 companies polled by Sheryl Sandberg's Lean In and McKinsey & Company in 2015:** "Women in the Workplace 2015," Lean In, McKinsey & Company, http://womenintheworkplace.com/ui/pdfs/Women _in_the_Workplace_2015.pdf?v=5.

Week 37: Take Studies, Recommendations, and (Especially) Books With a Grain of Salt

194 **Your baby is about twenty-one inches long from head to toe:** Curtis and Schuler, *Your Pregnancy Week By Week*, 529.

Index

advice
  asking for, 96–99
  common themes in, 211–212
  See also recommendations, evaluating
advocacy (for mother and child), 142–146
Aerosmith (band), 55
Affordable Care Act, 57
Agency for Health Care Research and Quality, 133
alcohol, during pregnancy, 64–65
Allen, Woody, 43
allergies, writing down mother's, 200
American Academy of Pediatrics (AAP)
  on alcohol intake during pregnancy, 64, 65
  on breast-feeding, 127, 131, 132, 133, 134, 135
  on television, 195–197

American Grown (Obama), 172
Angela (author's friend), 150
Animal Folk Songs for Children (album), 93
antianxiety medications, 61
antidepressants, 61
anxiety, information-induced, 26–29
Aqualung (album), 13
Argonaut (student newspaper), 34, 69
assistance
  do-it-yourself approach, 161–163
  from friends and family, 204–205
  offering to your lady, 30–32
  to the primary caregiver, 182–185
  See also chores
asthma, breast-feeding and, 136
Atlantic (magazine), 135
attention, undivided, 155–156

babymoons, 166–167

Babypants, Caspar. *See* Ballew, Chris

Bagley, Aaron, 78, 106–109, 177–178, 180

Bagley, Baxter, 106–109, 177–178

Bagley, Jessixa, 107, 108, 109, 178, 180

Ballew, Chris (Caspar Babypants), 96–99, 102

Band on the Run (album), 13

Basie, Count, 14

Basie Straight Ahead (album), 14

Beatles (band), 98

Beck, 67–69, 86

Ben (author's uncle), 170, 174

Benedikt, Allison, 28

Berninger, Matt, 56

Better Sex Video Series, The (DVD), 41

Bill (author's former roommate), 10, 170

birth plan, 200

birthing courses, 158–160

    best advice given by, 162

    best reason for attending, 159–160

    3x5 version of material, 156

Bjorns, 99

Blackwell, Ben, 70–74

Blackwell, Malissa, 70–71, 72, 73

Blackwell, Violet, 71, 72, 73

Blender (magazine), 16

bonding, 112, 134

books

    anxiety induced by, 26–29

    evaluating recommendations from, 194–198

Bowe, David, 140–141

breast cancer

    breast-feeding and, 134–135

    in men, 64

breast-feeding, 94, 125–137, 141

    claims and rebuttals, 132–136

    depression linked to failure of, 61, 129

    libido influenced by, 42

    pressure to provide, 125–130

    pumping, 127–129, 130, 135

"Breed" (song), 12–13

Brian (author's friend), 2, 4, 185

Brigham Young University, 189, 211

Bryce (author's friend), 5, 213

Buhner, Jay, 83

Bumbershoot, 67–70, 87–88,
    191
Bureau of Labor Statistics,
    173
Burton, Jane, 104, 105
Buying and Selling (television
    program), 9

Cake (band), 67, 76, 86
car-seat installation, 120–121
Casablancas, Julian, 97
"Case Against Breast-
    Feeding, The" (Rosin),
    135
Centers for Disease Control
    and Prevention (CDC),
    63, 64
Charles, Ray, 55–56
Charlotte (Tyler's and
    Chelsea's child), 116
cheeses, unpasteurized, 63–64
Chelsea (author's friend),
    114–115, 166
childbirth, 147–152
childcare arrangements,
    100–112
    during absences, 105–106
    daycare, 101–103
    nannies, 104–105
    primary caregiver and
        helper roles, 182–185
    Todd and Jamie Method,
        Part II, 109–110

childrearing
    common concerns and
        advice, 206–212
    essentials of, 153–157
    learning, 113–118
choline, in eggs, 175
chores
    doing extra, 94–95
    posthospital division of,
        205
    sex life correlated with, 41
    See also assistance
circumcision, 145–146
Clash, The (band), 177
cleaning out (your home),
    11–14
cleaning up (yourself), 1–5,
    213–215
Coleman, Vince, 83
Colen, Cynthia G., 136–137
Coltrane, John, 14
Coltrane, Scott, 74, 117–118,
    168, 190
Connery, Sean, 104
contractions, labor, 148, 149
cooking, 169–175
Cora, Joey, 83, 88
Cornell University, 175
Costa Concordia cruise ship
    disaster, 73–74
Creedence Clearwater (band),
    13
Crescent (album), 14

Crock-Pots, 169–174, 204
crying, soothing, 79–81

Dantas, Stella, 159–160
Dark Knight Rises, The (film), 105
daycare, 101–103
"Debra" (song), 69
deli meats, 63–64
depression, 58–61
  breast-feeding failure and, 61, 129
  prevalence of pre-and postpartum, 59
  symptoms of, 59, 60
"Devils Haircut" (song), 68
diabetes, diet and, 173, 175
diaper bags, 37–39, 203
diapers, disposable *vs.* reusable, 98
diet/nutrition
  babies' (*see* breast-feeding; formula-feeding)
  cooking and, 169–175
  during pregnancy, 62–65
  stocking up on food, 204
Dirtbombs (band), 70
doctor's appointments
  advocating for your lady at, 143–144
  importance of father's presence at, 159–160
  mentioning depressive

symptoms during, 60
  See also pediatricians
do-it-yourself approach, 161–163
Doors (band), 14
Dylan, Bob, 83
Dyson, James, 51

ear infections, breast-feeding and, 133
eggs, poaching, 175
Ellis, Jill, 178
Expecting Better (Oster), 65

Facebook, 190
Fat Kid Rules the World (film), 86–87
Filson factory store, 23–25, 34–37, 38, 46, 49, 51
fish, 65
food. *See* diet/nutrition
formula-feeding, 94, 124–137, 140
  breast-feeding compared with, 132–136
  disapproval of, 125–126
Franklin, Aaron, 209–210
Franklin, Aretha, 55
Franklin, Paul, 104–106, 211
Franklin Barbecue, 209
Frozen (soundtrack), 95

Gaffigan, Jim, 10

Gano, Graham, 195
garden-grown food,
    alternative to, 172–173
gastrointestinal infections,
    breast-feeding and,
    132–133
Gerardo (author's friend),
    53–55
Getz, Stan, 92
Getz/Gilberto (album), 92
"Girl From Ipanema, The"
    (song), 92
Goner Records, 72
Gonerfest, 72
Good Morning America
    (television program), 27
Griffey, Ken, Jr., 83, 88, 89–90
Griffin, Jim, 103, 209
Guns N' Roses (band), 48
gym, going to, 45–46

Hansard, Glen, 25
Happiest Baby on the Block
    (DVD), 80–81
healthychildren.org, 196
helicopter parents, 154–155
help. *See* assistance
Hill, David, 195–198
Hill, Jeff, 187–189, 211
Hill, Juanita, 187
home
    bigger-is-better fallacy,
    6–10

cleaning out, 11–14
"Homeward Bound" (song),
    13
hospitals
    list for the big day, 199–201
    prebirth tours of, 45, 125,
    200
hypertension, diet and, 175

IBM, 187–190
Interstellar (film), 104, 106, 211

Jackson 5 (musical group), 34
Joel, Billy, 92
Jones, Harold, 14
*Journal of the American Medical
    Association (JAMA)*, 132,
    133

Karp, Harvey, 80–81, 109
Keyes, Greg, 139, 154–157,
    159
Kimelman, Judy
    on breast- and formula-
    feeding, 129
    on childrearing, 212
    on information-induced
    anxiety, 27, 28, 29
KJR (radio station), 34
Knocked Up (film), 144, 148
Kornelis, Betsy, 3–5, 7, 8, 12,
    19, 45, 48, 49, 86, 90, 93,
    95, 97, 102, 111, 112, 170,

Kornelis, Betsy (*continued*)
  177, 178–181, 195, 203,
  214
  birthing courses and, 156
  Chris's advocacy for, 143,
    144, 146
  Chris's career decisions
    and, 16, 17, 20, 21, 22,
    52–53
  Chris's medical check-up
    and, 139–140
  feeding of babies and,
    125–128, 129–130
  help wish-list compiled by,
    31–32
  hospital stay of, 201
  during labor and
    childbirth, 148–152
  meets, moves in with, and
    marries Chris, 3–4
  as primary caregiver,
    183–184
  time alone with Chris, 160,
    165–166
Kornelis, Chris
  advocacy for mother and
    child, 143–146
  career choices and
    changes, 16–25, 34–37,
    48–53, 191–193
  cleaning himself up, 2–5,
    214–215

father of, 83–85, 88–90
grandfather of, 56
helping Betsy, 31–32,
  183–185
medical check-up for,
  139–140
mother of, 13, 85, 111,
  150–151
outings with Thomas,
  85–88, 191, 193
record collection of, 12–14
time alone with Thomas,
  111–112
Kornelis, Lucy, 7, 9, 14, 85,
  112, 120, 143, 177, 179,
  195, 198, 214
  Betsy's pregnancy with,
    31–32
  birth of, 149–152
  dad's first lessons in caring
    for, 163
  feeding of, 125–126,
    129–130
  parental division of care
    for, 183–184, 185
  swaddling of, 76, 78
Kornelis, Thomas, 2, 8, 19, 20,
  45, 74, 84, 90, 97, 125,
  144, 150, 151, 156, 166,
  167, 177, 179, 195, 203,
  214–215
  birth of, 148–149, 201

circumcision of, 145–146
dad's first lessons in caring
    for, 162–163
dad's outings with, 85–88,
    191, 193
dad's time alone with,
    111–112
dad's work schedule and,
    36, 48, 52–53
in daycare, 101–103
feeding of, 126–128, 140
music and, 12–13, 14, 92,
    93
parental division of care
    for, 183–184, 185
parental fallibility and,
    207–209
priority changes following
    birth of, 23–24

LA Weekly, 52
*League of Extraordinary
    Gentlemen, The* (film), 104
Lean In, 190
Lemagie, Susan, 212
Lennon, John, 13
Libby, Roger, 41–43, 168
Life360 app, 178
Lillard, Matthew, 86
listening (to children),
    155–156
listeriosis, 63–64

lists
    Betsy's for Chris, 31–32
    for the first days home,
        202–205
    for the hospital stay,
        199–201
London Calling (album), 177
love, 155, 157
lubricants, 42
Lullaby Renditions of Radiohead
    (album), 93
Lynch, Marshawn, 90

Marsalis, Branford, 24
masturbation, 43
maternity leave, 190
Maxim (magazine), 192
McConaughey, Matthew,
    104
McKagan, Duff, 48–49, 52, 84
McKinsey & Company, 190
Medium Field Bag (Filson),
    37–38
Meek, Joan, 131–132, 136
M83 (band), 70
Mercer Street Books, 108
mercury, in fish, 65
Meyers, David, 133
"Mom: The Designated
    Worrier" (Shulevitz),
    184–185
Moody, James, 24

Morning Phase (album), 69
Morrison, Jim, 14
Murdock, Sonia, 59–61
Murkoff, Heidi, 27, 28
music
    for children, 91–95
    keeping collections of,
        11–14

nannies, 104–105
National, The (band), 56
National Highway Traffic
    Safety Administration,
    121
National Institute of Child
    Health and
    Development, 103
National Institutes of Health,
    103, 209
Nelson, Willie, 55
Netflix, 190
Nevermind (album), 12
"New Pollution, The" (song),
    68
New York Times, 184
Newsweek, 172
Nirvana (band), 12, 85, 92
Norm (car seat installation
    instructor), 120–123

Obama, Barack, 172
Obama, Michelle, 172–173

obesity, childhood, 133, 172
    See also weight control
Ollie (Tyler's and Chelsea's
    child), 115, 116
omega-3 fatty acids, in fish,
    65
oral sex, 29, 43
Oster, Emily, 65
outings and getaways
    with your children, 82–90,
        191, 193
    with your spouse/partner,
        164–168

*Parsley, Sage, Rosemary and
    Thyme* (album), 13
part-time work, 190
paternity leave (and beyond),
    186–193
Patty (author's friend), 53–55
Patty's Mexican Kitchen,
    53–55
pediatricians, 138–141
perfectionism, avoiding, 94
Perry, Joe, 55
Phil, Dr., 109
poached eggs, 175
postpartum depression. *See*
    depression
Postpartum Resource Center,
    59
Poulsbo Music, 13

prebirth hospital tour, 45, 125, 200

prenatal check-ups. *See* doctor's appointments

prepregnancy courses. *See* birthing courses

Presidents of the United States of America (band), 97

Prince, 114

Radiohead (band), 18

Ramey, David M., 136

recommendations, evaluating, 194–198
See also advice

record collection, keeping, 11–14

Rich, Charlie, 86

Ritz, David, 55–56

Robert (author's friend), 68

Rolling Stone (magazine), 16–23, 56

Rosin, Hanna, 135

Roth, David Lee, 151

Rubber Soul (album), 13

Ruth (Norm's child), 123

safe words, 205

Sandberg, Sheryl, 190

Sandy Hook Elementary School shooting, 48

Sarow, Debbie, 108

Sasquatch! Music Festival, 69

Scream (film), 86

Sea Change (album), 69

Seahawks, 90, 195, 198

Seattle Mariners, 83, 87, 88–90

Seattle Weekly, 56
author's employment with, 16, 17, 18, 35, 107
author's termination from, 49–50, 192

Seeger, Peggy, 93

sex, 29
tips for, 40–43
work schedule and, 52

Shawn (author's friend), 17, 21

Shulevitz, Judith, 184–185

Simon, Paul, 83, 114

Simon & Garfunkel, 13

Skype, 105–106

Slate (magazine), 28

sleep promotion. *See* swaddling

"Smells Like Teen Spirit" (song), 12, 85

Smiler, Andrew, 171, 180, 205

Smith, Elliott, 14

SPIN (magazine), 16

Strokes, The (band), 97

studies, evaluating
 recommendations from,
 194–198
sudden infant death
 syndrome (SIDS),
 breast-feeding and, 135
Susan G. Komen for the Cure,
 134
swaddling, 75–78, 77(fig.), 80,
 81
Swedish Hospital, 45
Swell Season, The (duo),
 25
sympathy weight, 44–46

telecommuting, 189–190
television, 195–198
Third Man Records, 71, 72,
 73, 109
"Thrift Shop" (song), 36
time
 with your spouse/partner,
  160, 164–168
 for yourself, 176–181
Todd and Jamie Method,
 71–72
Todd and Jamie Method,
 Part II, 109–110
Tull, Jethro, 13
Tumble Bee (album), 92–93
Tyler (author's friend),
 114–116, 117, 166

United Kingdom, 129
University of Idaho, 2
University of Oregon, 74, 117,
 168, 190
"Uptown Girl" (song),
 92

vaccines, 141
Valentine, Jamie, 71–72,
 109–110
Valentine, Todd, 71–72, 74,
 109–110, 112
Valentine, Townes, 72, 74,
 109–110, 112
Van Halen (band), 151
Veirs, Laura, 91–95, 97
vests, weight camouflage
 with, 46
Village Voice, 52
Vince (author's friend),
 214–215
Virgin Megastore, 14

Waits, Tom, 183
Wall Street Journal, 51, 52, 53,
 178, 192
water, breaking of, 148, 152
weight control, 44–46
 See also obesity, childhood
What to Expect When You're
 Expecting (Murkoff),
 26–29

"Where It's At" (song), 67
White Stripes (band), 70–71, 73
Wings (band), 13
Wood, Barbara, 188–189
work
  balancing life with, 47–57, 114–116
  changing careers, 15–25, 114–116
  part-time, 190
  taking leave from, 186–193
  telecommuting, 189–190
World Health Organization (WHO), 132, 133
"worry work," 185

XO (album), 14

Zee, Ginger, 27